Steve Pye

PRACTICAL COMMUNICATION THEORY

Dave Adamy

LYNX Publishing
Sunnyvale, CA

Cover Design by Terry Fisk

LYNX Publishing
1587 Vireo Avenue
Sunnyvale, CA 94987
or
P.O. Box 70544
Sunnyvale, CA 94086-0544

International Standard Book Number: 1-885897-04-9
Library of Congress Catalog Card Number: 94-96238

ACKNOWLEDGEMENTS

It is an honor to acknowledge the contributions of the following individuals who took the time to review the draft of this book, both for technical accuracy and for appropriateness to the audience for whom it is intended. Each gave freely of his considerable expertise and insight, and each made suggestions which have significantly improved the book.

Dr. Timothy Healy

Professor Frederic Levien

Mr. Michael Licata

Mr. William Shellenberger

Mr. Gregory Wannamaker

Mr. Charles Weisman

Dr. Edward Wischmeyer

It is also appropriate to acknowledge the many anonymous individuals who have developed the nomographs and rules of thumb enjoyed by a whole generation of communications professionals. This kind of sharing with colleagues is what makes a profession a profession.

TABLE OF CONTENTS

TABLE OF CONTENTS (CONT.)

FOREWORD

The key to understanding many important fields … wireless communication, television broadcasting, radar, remote control, data links, and electronic warfare to name just a few … is a *practical* understanding of radio propagation. You probably don't care how radio waves propagate, but before you can specify or design any type of equipment that generates or receives radio signals -- or determine whether or not it will dependably do its job in a new situation -- you will need to be able to predict what a transmitted signal will "look like" when it gets to a receiver … as a function of frequency, distance, weather, and interference. This book will provide you with practical working tools to do just that -- without getting into the intimidating mathematical expressions with which these considerations are explained in most communication theory texts. *There are no integral signs in this book.*

This is a true story. As a junior systems engineer, I took a problem to the office of an internationally recognized communications expert. I don't remember the problem, but distinctly remember the answer. He started with Maxwell's equations and filled the blackboard with small print twice (elapsed time 40 minutes) before answering, "That's what I thought … it's about half a dB."

During the last half hour of the derivation process, I became more and more convinced that I didn't really want to know that badly … there just had to be an easier way to solve those "half a dB" problems that come up every day.

1

I soon learned about a wealth of practical "rules of thumb," charts and nomographs with which senior systems engineers went directly to the answers, without all of the stimulating math. During the intervening 30 years, I have collected these gems in a small, tattered notebook that has accompanied me through much of the world (*never* checked in luggage).

This book is a direct descendent of that precious, tattered notebook ... expanded with explanations ... checked by mathematical derivation when I was not completely confident of the accuracy or the limitations of a rule of thumb ... and corrected in a few (very few) cases. For completeness, it also includes some general descriptive information about communication links ... but even this is interspersed with those rules of thumb and handy charts.

I stand in awe of people who can look at an equation with multiple integral signs and see which way to change a variable to make a real life system work properly ... I am not one of them. Only after I understand what is going on in a physical sense, can I see and apply what the equation is trying to tell me. Therefore, devices and phenomena are described in physical rather than mathematical terms ... to avoid confusing you (and maybe me).

The explanations, formulas, charts and nomographs in this book are in general accurate to 1 dB -- which I have found over the years to be fully adequate for almost all system design and analysis tasks.

Sometimes, of course, more accurate answers are required -- involving blackboards dense with integral signs or computers cranking out ten digit numbers. But in these cases, I have always used the approaches presented in this book to be sure that the answer was *approximately* right.

When a detailed analysis gives an answer grossly different from my quick analysis, I ask for an explanation of the assumptions. Almost always, the deeply mathematical analysis is trying to break the laws of physics in some subtle way. When we fix the assumptions, and then solve the

2

problem we thought we were solving, the precise answers are consistent with the 1 dB answers. It is much better to fix that kind of problem *before* you freeze the design and spend a lot of money manufacturing something that is very hard to fix later.

Another very practical issue is explaining communication theory concepts in terms that the boss or the customer (who maybe used to be an engineer) will find understandable and useful. The equations in the form presented in this book, and the graphical explanations used should be very useful to you in that task.

You may already know much of the material presented in this book. However, in accordance with the principle that it is far better to repeat something you already know (and risk insulting the intelligence of some readers) than to leave something out (and have someone seriously confused), this book errs on the side of putting it in. Besides, most of us who have been out of school for a few years don't mind being reminded -- and we remember (with little kindness) those text authors who were overly fond of the phrase, "This is left as an exercise for the student."

On the other hand, every attempt is made to make it easy for you to skip to just the answer you need for the task at hand. For your convenience, all of the formulas and nomographs are repeated in appendixes at the end of the book. You should also have a laminated card with an overview of the link equation and references to backup material in the book. It was there when the book was shipped, but if yours has grown legs and walked away, write to the author (see the "about the author" page at the end of the book) for a replacement.

I hope you find the working tools in this book as useful as I have … and that they keep you out of as much trouble as they have me.

Dave Adamy

3

Chapter 1

INTRODUCTION

You, like most people, probably don't care about the mechanics of radio propagation. What everyone cares about is the quality of received signals – which we perceive as the fidelity of a voice signal, the clarity of a television image, the accuracy of a radar, or the dependability of a remote control command (among others). But adequate received signal quality is only achieved when all of the elements of the communication link are proper for the range and interference environment in which they must operate.

This book will allow you to select link components which will deliver the desired received signal quality ... or to determine the signal quality that will be achieved with a particular link ... or to determine the conditions (i.e. range and interference) for which a selected link will deliver adequate signal quality.

1.1   The Communication Link

The basic element of radio communication is a communication link as shown in Figure 1-1. It includes a transmitter, a receiver, transmitting and receiving antennas, and everything that happens to the radio signal as it passes between the two antennas.

The range of radio communication applications goes far beyond the simple case of one transmitter "talking" to one

Figure 1-1   Generic Communication Link

receiver. Some transmissions are broadcasts, intended for receipt by many listeners at greatly varying ranges. Some are received by unintended receivers in addition to the intended receiver, either as interference or as deliberate interception. In some cases, transmissions are designed to be reflected back to a receiver collocated with the transmitter. Some are designed to deliberately interfere with the reception of intended signals. However, every transmission from a transmitter to a receiver obeys the same laws of physics, so each of these cases can be analyzed -- one transmission path at a time -- using the same rules and formulas.

The focus of this book is on what happens to an information signal as it *passes through* the link. The link components are discussed functionally ... in terms of what each does to the signals passing through it ... rather than how they are implemented. Likewise, the various things that happen to signals as they propagate between the two antennas are discussed in terms of the net differences between the transmitted and received signals, with only as much discussion of the processes as necessary to allow you to understand what is happening.

Even if you are only specifying or supplying one of the link elements, you need to understand the whole link to do the job properly. Consider the broadcast situation shown in Figure 1-2. If you are providing only the transmitter, you will need to transmit adequate power to allow the farthest intended receiver to output your information signal with adequate quality, so you need to analyze the requirements of *that* link, making reasonable assumptions about the nature of the receiver to be used. If you are providing a receiver to receive that transmission, it must be able to perform adequately from the minimum design range to the maximum design range and to reject any interfering signals expected to be present, so you need to analyze the links from the transmitter to your receiver at minimum and maximum range. You also need to analyze the link from a worst case (or perhaps typical) interfering transmitter to determine the interference rejection specifications your receiver must meet.

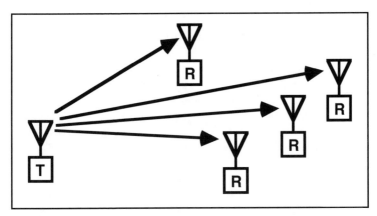

Figure 1-2 Broadcast Links

Now consider the unintended receiver situation of Figure 1-3. If you are providing the unintended receiver (for example, a monitoring receiver to be used by a government regulatory agency), you will need to analyze the link from the transmitter to the intended receiver to determine what parameters the transmitter must have to do its job. Then, you will need to analyze the link from the transmitter to your unintended receiver to determine the required specifications

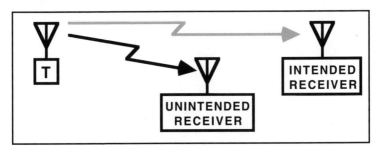

Figure 1-3 Unintended Receiver Link

1-3

for the receiver you employ. The unintended link can be quite different from the intended link if, for example, the transmitter uses a directional antenna pointed at its intended receiver or if your receiver is much closer or farther from the transmitter than the intended receiver.

1.2 A Few Important Definitions

Here are some definitions that are commonly used in the field, and that will be used throughout this book:

• **Information Signal** -- Any type of input to a transmitter that is intended for reproduction at the output of a distant receiver. This includes human voice, music, the video output of a television camera, a digital signal from a computer, a radar pulse, and many others. The whole purpose of communication is to deliver this signal.

• **Information Bandwidth** -- the amount of frequency spectrum that is required for the Information Signal to retain its proper function. Examples are, the amount of spectrum required for a human voice to be heard with adequate quality or the amount of spectrum required for a television signal to produce an adequate picture on the screen of a standard commercial television set.

• **Modulation Bandwidth** -- The highest modulating frequency. This is normally equal to the information bandwidth.

• **Transmission Bandwidth** -- The frequency spectrum occupied by the signal output by the transmitter.

• **Required Predetection Bandwidth** -- The spectrum that must be received in order for a receiver to do its job. This is often equal to the transmission bandwidth, but not always. Sometimes, a receiver does not have to accept the full transmitted bandwidth of a signal to do its job. There are also circumstances in which the receiver must be wider than the transmission bandwidth of the received signal to do its job.

• **RF Frequency** -- Literally, the "radio frequency" frequency of a transmitted signal ... not very good English, but commonly used to distinguish the actual transmission frequency from intermediate frequency (IF) or audio frequency.

• **Ether (or Ether Waves)** – This is an archaic term identifying the substance that was thought to pervade all of space. It is starting to come back in discussions of radio propagation as a term which includes any atmosphere (the Earth or any other planet) and the vacuum of space.

1.3   Assumptions

The top level assumptions made in this book are the following:

• Unless stated otherwise, we will assume that the designers of equipment knew what they were doing. That is, receivers have the optimum bandwidth, transmitters use the most efficient techniques, processors use optimum algorithms, antennas have the normally expected efficiency, etc.

• Except in Chapter 7, we will deal with "line of sight" communications -- that is the transmitting and receiving antennas "see" each other over an unobstructed straight line.

• We will be using many expressions involving the logarithm (abbreviated "log") of a number. There are other types of logs (e.g. natural log or log to the base 2) – but in this book, "log" always means log to the base 10 (which is what you get when you punch the "log" key on your scientific calculator).

• Unless otherwise stated, noise is assumed to be "white," Gaussian noise: That is with its amplitude probability normally distributed about zero and its power density evenly distributed over the whole bandwidth considered.

1.4   Scope of the Book

The main subjects covered in this book are:

• Decibel (dB) forms of values and equations (Chapter 2)

• Signal to noise ratio – its definition and how it applies to communication theory (Chapter 3)

• The communication link – the characteristics and role of each part of the link (Chapter 4)

• The Link Equation – predicting the performance of line of sight links in good weather (Chapter 5)

• Receiver System Sensitivity – calculation of the sensitivity achieved by a wide range of types of receiving systems (Chapter 6)

• Challenging propagation conditions – characterizing and predicting link performance in bad weather, when there is not quite line of sight, or when either the transmitter or receiver is moving. (Chapter 7)

Each of these subjects will be covered to adequate depth to allow you to use the techniques taught to predict the performance of a radio link.

Appendixes

Derivations are generally left out of the body of the book to preserve the flow. Where appropriate, the derivations are presented in Appendixes A and B.

Finally, there are four "quick formula" appendixes which contain all of the formulas and, nomographs in Chapters 4, 5, 6, and 7. In the chapters, all equations and nomographs are explained in detail, and are illustrated with examples. Once you understand how to use them, you'll save much "page flipping" time by getting just the formula or nomograph you need from the appropriate appendix.

For consistency, metric units are used throughout the chapters of this book. However, for your convenience in dealing with requirements which define distance in statute miles or nautical miles and antenna diameter or obstruction height in feet, the quick formula appendixes also contain formulas and nomographs in those units.

Chapter 2

ABOUT dB

Note: If you already speak fluent dB, please feel free to skip most of this chapter ... just check out the tables and the "book keeping" diagram methodology, we'll be using them later.

In communication theory, we spend a lot of time manipulating widely varying signal strength values. We also deal with non-integer powers and roots of numbers. The use of decibel (or dB) forms of numbers and equations greatly simplifies dealing with both of these considerations.

Any number expressed in dB is logarithmic, which makes it convenient to compare values which may differ by many orders of magnitude. (Note that numbers in non-dB form are called "linear" to differentiate them from the logarithmic dB numbers.) Numbers in dB form also have the great charm of being easy to manipulate :

- To multiply linear numbers, you add their logarithms

- To divide linear numbers, you subtract their logarithms

- To raise a linear number to the nth power, you multiply its logarithm by n

- To take the nth root of a linear number, you divide its logarithm by n

To take maximum advantage of this convenience, it is common to put numbers into dB form as early in the process as possible ... and to convert them back to linear forms as late as possible (if at all). In many cases, the most commonly used forms of answers remain in dB, so we can avoid converting back to linear forms altogether.

It is important to understand that any value expressed in dB units must be a *ratio* (which has been converted to logarithmic form). Common examples are:

- Amplifier gain (i.e. the ratio of the output signal strength to the input signal strength).

- Antenna gain (also treated like an amplification ratio, but with some qualifiers).

- Losses (i.e. signal attenuation ratio) when passing through:
  - cables.
  - switches. (The off position of course has much more attenuation than the on position, but the on position still has some loss.)
  - power dividers (i.e. ratio of signal power at each output port to input power).
  - filters.

To create useful equations in dB form, it is necessary to express absolute values as dB numbers. Signal strength in units of "dBm" is the most common example. Since dB values must always be ratios, a trick is required. The trick is to calculate the *ratio* of the desired absolute value to some fixed value and then convert that ratio to dB form. For example, signal strength in dBm is the dB form of the ratio of that signal strength to one milliwatt. (More on that later.)

2.1 Conversion to dB form

The basic formula for conversion into dB is:

Ratio (in dB) = 10 log(Linear Ratio)

for example, 2 (the ratio of 2 to 1) converts to dB form as:

10 log(2) = 3 dB

(OK, so it's actually 3.0103 dB … give me a break, everyone rounds it to 3 dB)

and 1/2 (i.e. 0.5) becomes:

10 log(0.5) = -3 dB

To make the conversion the easy way (using a calculator, of course), it will have to be a scientific calculator which has log and 10^x functions.

To convert into dB

- **Enter the linear ratio (for example, 2)**

- **Press the "log" key**

- **Multiply by 10**

- **Read the answer in dB (3.0103, which rounds to 3)**

To convert back from dB form to linear form, the formula is:

$$\text{Linear Ratio} = 10^{\left(\frac{\text{Ratio in dB}}{10}\right)}$$

For example:

$$10^{(3/10)} = 10^{0.3} = 2$$

Again the easy way … using the calculator.

To convert dB values back to linear form:

- **Enter the dB value (for example, 3)**

- **Divide by 10 (Then hit "=" to get the value onto the display.)**

- **Press the "10^X" key**
  (On many calculators this is the
  second function on the log key.)

- **Read the answer as the linear ratio
  (1.99526, which rounds to 2)**

2.2 Absolute Values in dB Form

As stated above, the most common example of an absolute value expressed in dB form is *signal strength* in dBm. This is the ratio of the signal power to 1 milliwatt – converted to dB form exactly as shown in Section 2.1.

Note: dBm is a particularly important unit because many important formulas in the heart of this book either start or end (or both) with dBm values of signal strength.

For example, converting 4 Watts to dBm:

$$4 \text{ Watts} = 4{,}000 \text{ milliwatts}$$

$$10 \log(4000) = 36 \text{ dBm}$$

and, of course,

$$10^{36/10} = 10^{3.6} = 4000 \text{ (milliwatts)}$$
$$= 4 \text{ Watts}$$

2.3 dB Forms of Equations

dB form equations use absolute numbers (usually in dBm) and ratios (in dB). A typical equation includes: only one element in dBm on each side (modified by any number of ratios in dB), or only ratios in dB, or differences of two dBm values (which become dB ratios). One of the simplest dB form equations is illustrated by the amplifier in Figure 2-1, which multiplies input signals by a "gain" factor.

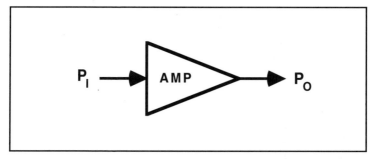

Figure 2-1 Amplifier

The linear form of the "amplifier" equation is:

$$P_O = P_I \times G$$

Where P_O is the output power, P_I is the input
power and G is the gain of the amplifier.

Both power numbers are in linear units (for example
milliwatts), and G is the gain factor in linear form (for
example 100). If the input power is 1 milliwatt, an amplifier
gain of 100 will cause a 100 milliwatt output signal.

By converting the input power to dBm and the gain
to dB, the equation becomes:

$$P_O = P_I + G$$

The output power is now expressed in dBm. Using the
same numbers, 1 milliwatt becomes 0 dBm, the gain
becomes 20 dB, and the output power is +20 dBm. (This
can be converted back to 100 milliwatts in linear units if
required).

This is a very simple case, in which the marginally
simpler calculation does not seem worth the trouble to
convert to and from dB forms. But now, consider a typical
communication theory equation. As will be shown in
Chapter 5, a transmitted signal is reduced by a "spreading
loss" which is proportional to the square of its frequency (F)
and the square of the distance (d) it travels from the

transmitting antenna. Thus the spreading loss is the product of F squared, d squared, and a constant (which includes several terms from the derivation). The formula is then:

$$L = K \times F^2 \times d^2$$

In dB form, F (dB) becomes 10 log(F). F^2 is 2[10 log (F)] or 20 log(F), and d^2 is transformed to 20 log(d) the same way. The constant is also converted to dB form, but first it is modified with conversion factors to allow us to input values in the most convenient units and generate an answer in the most convenient units. In this case, K is multiplied by the necessary conversion factors to allow frequency to be input in MHz and distance to be input in kilometers. When the log of this whole mess is multiplied by 10, it becomes 32.44 -- which is commonly rounded to 32. The spreading loss in dB can then be found directly from the expression:

$$L_S = 32 + 20 \log(F) + 20 \log(d)$$

Where: L_S = Spreading loss (in dB)
F = Frequency (in MHz)
d = Distance (in km)

which most people find much easier to use in practical applications. In later chapters, dB equations for all of the communication link relationships will be presented.

It is important to understand the role of the constant in this type of equation. Since it contains unit conversion factors, this equation only works if you input values in the proper units. In this book, the units for each term are given right below the dB equation -- every time. You will memorize some of these equations and use them often; be sure you also remember the applicable units.

2.4   Quick Conversions to dB Values

Table 2-1 gives some common dB values with their equivalent linear ratios. For example, multiplying a linear number by a factor of 1.25 is the same as adding 1 dB to the same number in dB form. (1 milliwatt x 1.25 is the same as 0 dBm + 1 dB -- so 1.25 milliwatts = 1 dBm).

Table 2-1 Common dB Values

Ratio	dB Value	Ratio	dB Value
1/10	-10	1.25	+1
1/4	-6	2	+3
1/2	-3	4	+6
1	0	10	+10

This table is extremely useful, because it will allow you to make quick determinations of approximate dB values without touching a calculator. Here's how it works:

- First, get from one (1) to the proper order of magnitude. This is easy, because each time you multiply the linear value by 10 you just add 10 dB to its dB value. Likewise, dividing by 10 subtracts 10 dB from the dB value.

- Then, use the ratios from Table 2-1 to get close to the desired number.

For example, 400 is 10 x 10 x 4. In dB form, these manipulations are 10 dB + 10 dB + 6 dB. A more common way to look at the manipulation is:

400 is: 20 dB (which gets you to 100)
                + 6 dB (to multiply by 4).
                = 26 dB

and 500 is approximately: 30 dB (= 1000)
                              - 3 dB (to divide by 2)
                              = 27 dB

Be careful not to be confused by "0 dB." A high ranking government official once embarrassed himself in a large meeting by announcing that, "The signal is completely gone when the signal to noise ratio gets down to 0 dB."

In fact, a 0 dB ratio between two numbers just means that they are equal to each other (i.e. have a ratio of 1).

Table 2-2 shows the power in dBm for various linear power values. This is a very useful table, and we will use these values many times in examples in later chapters.

Table 2-2 Signal Strength Levels in dBm

dBm	Signal Strength	dBm	Signal Strength
+90	1 Megawatt	+20	100 milliwatts
+80	100 Kilowatts	+10	10 milliwatts
+70	10 Kilowatts	0	1 milliwatt
+60	1 Kilowatt	-10	100 microwatts
+50	100 Watts	-20	10 microwatts
+40	10 Watts	-30	1 microwatt
+30	1 Watt		

Other values that are often expressed in dB form are shown in Table 2-3.

Table 2-3 Common dB Definitions

dBm	= dB value of $\dfrac{\text{Power}}{\text{1 milliwatt}}$
dBw	= dB value of $\dfrac{\text{Power}}{\text{1 Watt}}$
dBsm	= dB value of $\dfrac{\text{Area*}}{\text{1 square meter}}$
dBi	= dB value of antenna gain relative to that of an isotropic antenna**

* Commonly used for Antenna Area and Radar Cross Section
** See Section 4.4.1

2-8

One More Chance to be Seriously Confused about dBs

Voltage ratios are often expressed in dB, but it is common to convert the linear voltage ratio to dB using the formula:

**Voltage Ratio (in dB)
= 20 log (Linear Voltage Ratio)**

The basis for this practice is that the ratio of two power levels is equivalent to the ratio of the squares of two voltage levels (because $P = V^2/R$).

No voltage ratios will be expressed in dB in this book.

2.5   dB Book Keeping Diagrams

It is easy to become confused when manipulating gains, losses and signal strength levels in the various communications equations. Since the dB forms of equations typically involve addition and subtraction, they can be illustrated using simple diagrams which many people (enthusiastically including the author) find helpful in avoiding confusion. Through the rest of the book, small "dB book keeping" diagrams like this one will be inserted in the paragraphs in which the equations they represent are discussed. Wherever practical, the diagrams will be placed right with the equations they illustrate as shown in Figure 2-2.

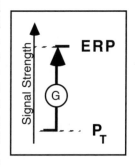

The dB book keeping diagrams will not be dignified with figure numbers, and usually will not be discussed. Their purpose is to help you keep "what is happening" in perspective.

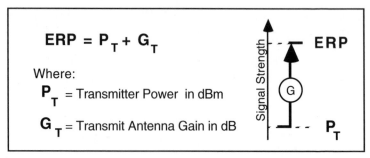

$$ERP = P_T + G_T$$

Where:

P_T = Transmitter Power in dBm

G_T = Transmit Antenna Gain in dB

Figure 2-2   dB equation with "book keeping" diagram

In every such diagram:

• Terms of the equation which are signal strength values are represented by horizontal lines.

• Terms of the equation which cause changes in signal strength are vertical arrows (pointing in the direction that the signal strength is changed by that term of the equation).

• The "action" in the diagram moves from left to right as you move through the right side of the equation.

• If the "answer" term of the equation (on the left side) is a ratio of signal strengths, it is shown as a vertical double headed arrow.

• If the "answer" term is a signal strength, it is shown as the final horizontal line in the diagram.

• All signal strength levels are in dBm and all changes in signal strength levels are in dB.

• No attempt is made to draw the signal strength values to scale, only the relative positions are significant.

Some people really like these diagrams, and some people don't. If you are in the latter group, please feel free to ignore them in good health. You purchased this book, and the customer is always right.

Chapter 3

SIGNAL TO NOISE RATIO

In considering communication link performance, signal to noise ratio (SNR) is an extremely important concept. It is the common way to *quantify* the *quality* of the signal at any point in the communication process. Ultimately, it is the signal to noise ratio that determines whether or not adequate communication takes place, but as will be seen in later chapters, the signal to noise ratio required at each point in the link depends on many factors.

3.1 Noise

Whole books are written on the nature of noise and its mathematical characterization, but it is sufficient for our purposes to define noise as random signals which are present along with desired signals in any communication channel. In many specifications, any non-random but undesired signals present in a circuit are also considered to be noise – particularly if they cannot be predicted, or if there are several which intermodulate in interesting ways. In this book, we won't call them noise unless they are non-coherent and must be considered present over a bandwidth greater than that in which we measure them.

There are two types of noise we will consider, thermal and man-made. Thermal noise comes from molecular activity in the atmosphere and in the materials from which the receiver is manufactured. The power of the thermal noise in an ideal circuit is calculated by the expression "kTB." As discussed in detail in Chapter 6, kTB is the product of Boltzman's constant, the temperature (in degrees K), and the bandwidth in which it is measured. Chapter 6 also discusses thermal noise in non-ideal circuits.

There are always interfering signals from inside and outside the receiver. These include ripple from power supply voltages, and conducted and radiated electromagnetic interference (EMI). Good design practice normally calls for all of these undesired signals to be lower than the thermal noise. However, if that is impossible or impractical, they will diminish the quality of the signal being communicated. While they are not literally noise, they are often difficult to distinguish from noise and are therefore often included in the noise part of the signal to noise ratio as discussed above.

External noise and interference signals are received by the receiving antenna along with desired signals. Interfering signals (deliberate or accidental) are discussed in Section 5.4. They are not considered in the noise part of the SNR, and must usually be dealt with individually.

External noise is the sum of all of the radio frequency emissions, both natural and man-made that reach the receiving antenna (except those we consider individually as interfering signals). If the receiver is very near a large noise generator (for example the engine in a motor vehicle) this particular source can be (and usually must be) reduced by filtering at its source or avoided through some operational approach (like turning the engine off when we want to operate the receiver). There is also a level of general background noise which is always present. Section 3.4 includes a chart quantifying this noise as a function of frequency and type of location (urban, suburban, or rural).

3.2   Signal to Noise Ratio

The signal to noise ratio is defined as the ratio of the signal power to the noise power (from all sources). The absolute levels of signal and noise are normally stated in dBm, so the ratio of the two levels (the signal to noise ratio) is in dB. For example, if the signal power (**S**) were

-104 dBm and the noise power (**N**) were -114 dBm, the signal to noise ratio (**SNR**) would be 10 dB. The signal to noise *ratio* (SNR) in dB is the difference of the signal and the noise powers (rather than the quotient) because both are in dBm (i.e. logarithmic numbers).

In the real world, there is no such thing as a pure signal – you can only measure a signal along with some level of noise. When you think you are seeing a pure signal, it is just that the signal to noise ratio is so large that you cannot detect the noise.

Figure 3-1 shows a signal with noise – in the time domain, as it would appear on an oscilloscope. The noise appears "fuzzy" on the oscilloscope because it is jittering in both time and amplitude from sweep to sweep. The image of noise on a oscilloscope is often called "the grass."

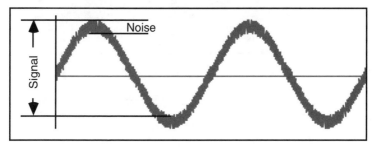

Figure 3-1   Signal with noise in time domain

This figure shows a fairly large signal to noise ratio which means that the signal is easily processed. If an audio signal had the signal to noise ratio depicted, the noise would be perceptible to a listener but not objectionable. Good enough to understand speech, but less than "high fidelity."

Figure 3-2 shows the same signal in the frequency domain (as it would appear on a spectrum analyzer). Again, the noise part of the display will appear "fuzzy" because it jitters in both frequency and amplitude.

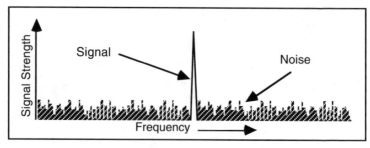

Figure 3-2 Signal with noise in frequency domain

Figure 3-3 shows a much lower signal to noise ratio (in the time domain), and Figure 3-4 shows the same signal with its associated noise in the frequency domain.

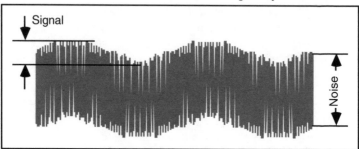

Figure 3-3 Lower SNR in time domain

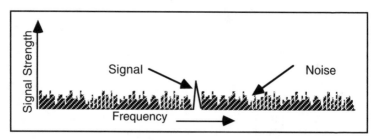

Figure 3-4 Same signal in frequency domain

In a communication system, the signal to noise ratio of the received signal can be no better than that in the transmitted signal, but transmitters are designed to output very high signal to noise ratios, so we will be mainly concerned about noise added to the signal by the receiver itself and transmitted into the receiving antenna from other sources.

3.3   Other Related Ratios

Some types of modulation provide improvement in signal to noise ratio for output signals -- relative to the SNR of the radio frequency signals that are received. Two important examples are frequency modulated signals and digital signals. In both cases, two "signal to noise" values must be considered, the output signal to noise ratio (SNR) and the RF SNR – which can be significantly different.

3.3.1 RF SNR

For frequency modulated or digitized signals, the "signal to noise ratio" (SNR) is normally taken to mean the output audio or video signal to noise ratio. In this book, the signal to noise ratio of the actual radio frequency signal received is called the RF signal to noise ratio (RF SNR). Some text books call it the "carrier to noise ratio" (CNR). (See Figure 3-5.) As will be shown in Chapter 6, the output signal to noise ratio of frequency modulated signals can be greatly improved from the RF SNR as a function of the frequency modulation index as long as the RF SNR is above a threshold level. The output SNR of digitally modulated signals is primarily the signal to quantization ratio (SQR) (see below), and is only secondarily related to the RF SNR.

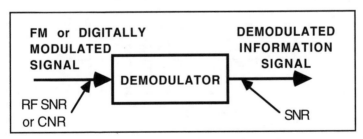

Figure 3-5   RF SNR or CNR vs. SNR

3.3.2 Signal to Quantization Ratio

The signal to quantization ratio (SQR) is the ratio of the signal amplitude to the quantization increment as shown in Figure 3-6. When an analog signal (for example a voice channel) is digitized, an analog to digital converter (ADC) compares it to a series of thresholds and generates a set of digital signals (ones and zeros) to describe the time history of the waveform digitized. The signal is transmitted as a digital bit stream. When the analog signal is reconstructed by a digital to analog converter (DAC), it is not a smooth curve, but jumps between defined levels as shown in Figure 3-6. The number of these levels is a function of the number of bits used in the digitization of each signal level. The non-smoothness of the reconstructed signal is usually called "Quantization Noise." The output signal quality is then properly specified as the "signal to quantization noise ratio" … however it is often called just the "signal to noise ratio."

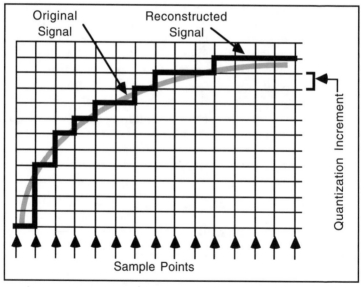

Figure 3-6 The effect of quantizing a signal

It is important to understand that this quantization noise is completely independent of the signal to noise ratio of the received RF signal. As will be shown in Chapter 6, the

RF SNR determines the *bit error rate* in the received digital signal, but the SQR is set in the original digitizing process. One of the great charms of digital communication systems is that the SQR remains constant even if the signal is subjected to many processing steps, whereas non-digitized signals tend to be degraded by every processing step. Section 6.3.3 includes a formula to determine signal to quantization noise ratio as a function of the number of bits per sample.

Naturally, the signal cannot be properly reproduced by the receiver unless it detects the proper bits, so the bit error rate is also important, and that does depend on the RF SNR. Section 6.3.3, presents curves of the bit error rates as a function of RF SNR for various modulation schemes.

3.4 Background Noise

Figure 3-7 is a characterization of the total, non-thermal background noise that will be seen by an omni-directional antenna in various types of locations. This is the electronic noise from street cars, automobile and truck engines, electric motors, high order intermodulations of hundreds of unrelated radio transmissions, and noise from outer space.

The chart shows the expected background noise in terms of dB above ideal thermal noise in a receiver of any specified bandwidth (called "dB above kTB" in the figure).

In Chapter 6 (Section 6.1) formulas and a graph are provided to determine the actual noise power of kTB in terms of temperature and bandwidth. After calculating kTB, the level of background noise power reaching an antenna can be determined from the appropriate lines on the graph.

The three lines on the chart show the expected noise power level for urban locations, suburban locations, and very quiet rural locations in which the noise is primarily cosmic.

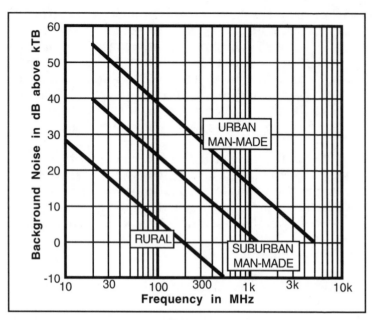

Figure 3-7 Background noise

It must be emphasized that these curves are average values, based on two different sources which combined data from many surveys, and with much smoothing of data. (The data varies by as much as 10 dB between the two sources.) All of the source data was collected using omnidirectional antennas. While impossible to predict with precision, the expected background noise can be an important system design parameter, particularly at low frequencies, where it may become dominant over the internal system noise of very sensitive receivers.

For an example calculation of the background noise level, consider a receiver with a 1 MHz bandwidth. Its kTB level (see Chapter 6) would be -114 dBm. If operated in a noisy urban area at 100 MHz using an omnidirectional antenna, this receiver would expect to receive a background noise level of - 76 dBm (-114 dBm + 38 dB).

Chapter 4

THE COMMUNICATION LINK

The communication link is everything required to get information signals from one point to another without wires. In its simplest form, as shown in Figure 4-1, the link includes a transmitter, a receiver, transmitting and receiving antennas, and everything that happens to the radio signals between the two.

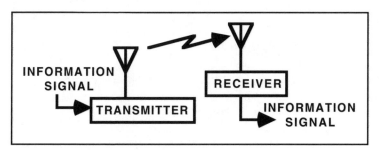

Figure 4-1   Elements of the Communication Link

This chapter provides functional descriptions of each of these link elements and also of the information signals which links are designed to carry.

4.1   Information Signals

The information signal carries the information to be communicated over the link. Information signals come in a bewildering variety of forms, but the most common are audio signals, digital data, and video signals.

Each of these types of information signals can be characterized by its information bandwidth and the output signal to noise ratio it requires to assure its adequate communication to the information user at the other end of the link. Table 4-1 shows each of these basic types along with some common subtypes and the demands each places on the communication link.

Table 4-1 Information Signals

Type of Signal	Typical Info Bandwidth	Typical SNR Required
Audio (Voice)	4 kHz	10 to 20 dB
Audio (Music)	15 kHz	20 to 40 dB
Digital Data	<1 Hz to >1GHz	10 to 20 dB
Video (Television)	4 MHz	40 dB or more
Video (Multichannel)	20 kHz to 4 GHz	10 to 20 dB
Video (Pulse)	0.1 to 10 MHz	10 to 20 dB

4.1.1 Audio Signals

Audio signals typically include human voice, music, or other audible sounds. They are limited in bandwidth to match the frequency response of the human ear.

Voice signals for communication must have adequate bandwidth for a human to receive the information passed. The most common example is a telephone circuit, which typically accepts an input band from 300 to 3,400 Hz. This frequency range allows us to easily understand what is being said and to recognize the voice of the speaker, but it clearly limits the quality of the output, and is not nearly adequate to pass music. Military communication networks can, if necessary, use even narrower bandwidth because of the disciplined vocabulary used by military communicators.

Music requires adequate bandwidth to reproduce the tonal qualities of singing voices and musical instruments. high fidelity music transmission requires a frequency range covering from less than 10 Hz to above fifteen kilohertz for "concert hall realism."

A special case audio signal (the first used in radio communication) is single tone Morse code. Morse code signals are typically generated by turning the RF carrier on and off. This is called "on-off-keyed" or OOK modulation, which is very narrow in bandwidth. The actual beeps heard by the receiving operator are generated in the receiver when the signal is present.

4.1.2 Digital Data

Digital data is a series of "ones" and "zeros" which form binary codes to represent numbers, letters, and graphical data. Computers talk to each other digitally, but there are also many other devices which input or output controls or data in digital form. Each one or zero is a "bit." Although digital data can be formatted in many ways, it is normally collected into 8-bit "bytes." Bytes are typically collected into frames and subframes which include synchronization provisions to allow the user of the data to identify individual bits and bytes in long data streams. (See Figure 4-2.) The synchronization signals are most often transmitted as extra bits. These synchronization bits, and other bits which are added to designate an intended user or to allow error detection and correction, are often referred to as "overhead" since the transmission medium must have enough throughput capacity to pass them, but they carry no direct signal information.

For transmission, digital data is typically formatted in "serial" form, that is one bit at a time (rather than in parallel form with each bit in a byte having its own wire, as is often the case inside of hardware). However, there are more complex modulation schemes, for example quadriphase-shift keying (QPSK), in which more than one simultaneous bit can be present in a single signal.

Digital signals have widely varying bandwidth, from much less than 1 Hz to Gigabit rates (more than 10^9 bits/sec). The signal bandwidth depends on the bit rate, which is in turn dictated by the amount and fidelity of information which must be transmitted per unit time.

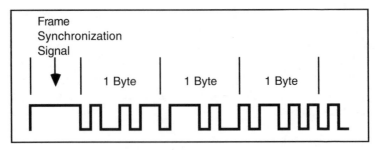

Figure 4-2   Digital Data Stream

4.1.3 Video Signals

Video signals convey information which must be changed to another form before it can be perceived by people or computers. The most common video signals carry broadcast television picture information. These signals have 4 MHz bandwidth and contain all of the information required to allow synchronization of the TV frame, and to set the brightness and color of each dot on the screen. Figure 4-3 shows the structure of the television signal as a function of frequency, and Figure 4-4 shows it as a function of time.

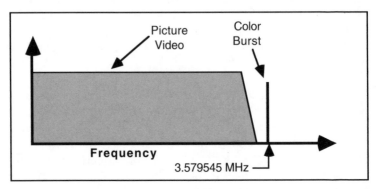

Figure 4-3   Television Video Signal in
Frequency Domain

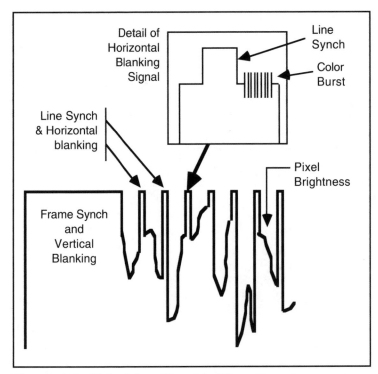

Figure 4-4 Television Signal in Time Domain

Another type of video signal contains many audio channels which are multiplexed into one signal so they can be transmitted together. (See Figure 4-5.) These "multichannel" signals are used in microwave telephone links, and a few other applications. The video bandwidth is typically 4 kHz per voice channel slot. The individual voice grade channels are input to a modulator which creates the video signal to drive the transmitter, and are demodulated and distributed after being output from a receiver.

A third type of video signal is pulsed. As shown in Figure 4-6, pulses are short duration signals which are used to abruptly turn the transmitter on and off, generating short bursts of radio frequency energy. The most common use of pulsed signals is in radars. Typical information bandwidths for pulse signals are from 100 kHz to 10 MHz.

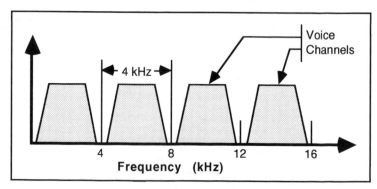

Figure 4-5 Multi-channel Video Signal

The bandwidth of a pulse signal is determined by the width of the pulse ... the shorter the pulse, the wider the bandwidth. Adequate bandwidth is often taken to be "one over the pulse width," for example, a 1 μsecond long pulse would require 1 MHz of bandwidth. However, the full spectrum occupancy of a nice square pulse includes many harmonics. The actual transmission bandwidth required will depend on the performance specifications of the radar generating the signal.

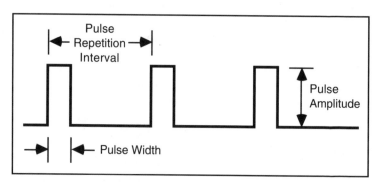

Figure 4-6 Pulse Signal

The receiver can narrow the bandwidth to improve sensitivity, but the shape of the received pulse depends on the narrowest filter it passes through. Figure 4-8 shows the shape of a pulse after various levels of filtering. Any of these shapes may be optimum, depending on the situation and the post detection processing applied to the signal.

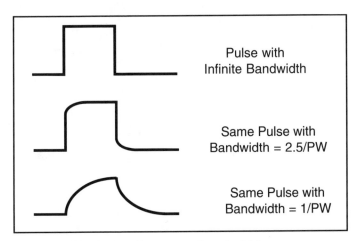

Figure 4-7   Pulse Shape vs. Bandwidth

4.2   Transmitters

Transmitters accept information inputs from various sources (people, computers, sensors, etc.) and convert them into forms which can be transmitted.

The transmitter output is characterized by its transmission bandwidth (in some units of frequency) and its power level (which is often stated in watts or kilowatts, but can be converted into dBm for convenience in link performance calculations).

Figure 4-8 shows a block diagram of a generalized transmitter. The actual circuitry required to implement each of these blocks varies widely, and is covered in detail in many communication theory texts. Our purpose here is just to deal with them functionally – describing what each block does, rather than how it does it.

4.2.1 Oscillator

The oscillator generates a "carrier signal" onto which the input information is modulated. The oscillator sets the radio frequency of the transmitted signal (often called the RF frequency to distinguish it from modulating frequencies).

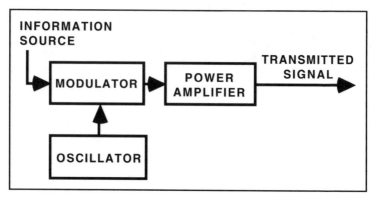

Figure 4-8 Transmitter Components

The use of radio frequencies is controlled by a set of national and international agreements to minimize interference among the many people trying to communicate. This is necessary because two or more signals at the same frequency in the same general area will interfere with each other.

Transmission frequencies are broken into bands which have a variety of names, as shown in Figure 4-9. These band names have been developed as a convenient way to specify and discuss hardware, for example an "S-band amplifier" or a "J-band radar." When in doubt, it is best to specify an RF frequency or frequency range directly in units of frequency (Hz, kHz, MHz or GHz). Table 4-2 describes the typical communications uses and characteristics of the various frequency ranges.

Table 4-2 Frequency Ranges

Frequency Range	Abbreviation	Type of Communication and Characteristics
Very Low, Low & Medium Frequency 3 kHz to 3 MHz	VLF LF MF	Very long range communication (ships at sea, etc.) Ground Waves circle earth
High Frequency 3 to 30 MHz	HF	Over the horizon communication Commercial AM Radio Signals reflect from Ionosphere
Very High Freq. 30 to 300 MHz	VHF	Mobile Communication, TV and Commercial FM Radio Line of sight required
Ultra High Freq. 300 MHz to 1 GHz	UHF	Mobile Communication, TV Line of sight required
Microwave 1 to 30 GHz	μw	TV and Telephone Links, Satellite Communication, Radar Line of sight required
Millimeter Wave 30 to 100 GHz	MMW	Radars. Requires line of sight High absorption in rain and fog

4.2.2 Modulator

The modulator modulates the input information signal onto the radio frequency carrier for transmission. The main characteristics of the modulation which affect the communication link performance are the amount of frequency spectrum that the modulated signal occupies and any signal to noise improvement factor.

The following types of modulation are the most common. Each is described in terms of its typical applications and its impact on link performance. There are many other modulation schemes, but most can be quite accurately characterized by their similarity to those described here.

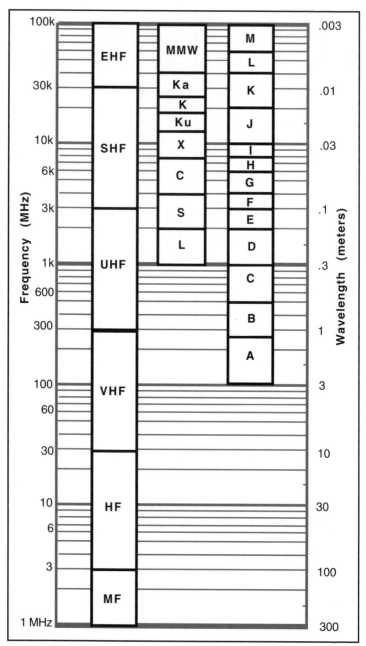

Figure 4-9 Frequency Bands

Amplitude Modulation

Amplitude modulation (AM), as shown in the time domain in Figure 4-10, carries the information signal as a series of variations in the amplitude (hence the transmitted power level) of the carrier. Figure 4-11 shows an AM signal in the frequency domain. The information signal is carried in two sidebands, which causes the spectrum occupancy to be approximately twice the information bandwidth. A detected AM signal typically provides a signal to noise ratio equal to the RF signal to noise ratio.

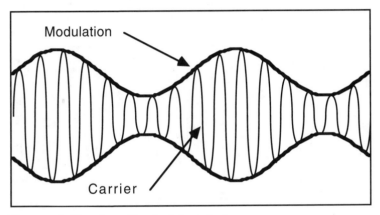

Figure 4-10   Amplitude Modulation

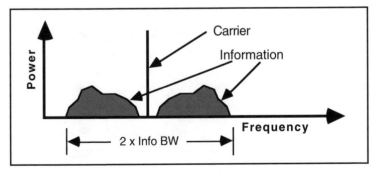

Figure 4-11   AM Signal in Frequency Domain

Frequency Modulation

Frequency modulation (FM), as shown in the time domain in Figure 4-12, carries the information signal as a series of variations in the frequency of the carrier. Figure 4-13 shows an FM signal in the frequency domain. Like AM, FM signals have two information carrying sidebands. However, the side-bands can occupy much more frequency spectrum because the amount of frequency variation can be several times the information bandwidth. The ratio of the transmitted frequency variation to the modulating frequency is called the modulation index (ß). The ratio of the peak frequency deviation to the information bandwidth is also ß.

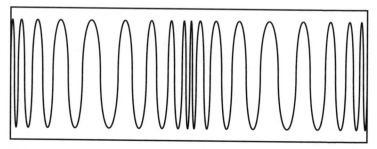

Figure 4-12 Frequency Modulation

The total frequency band required to transmit an FM signal is a non-linear function of the modulation index, but is typically set at:

$$BW_{FM} = 2 \times \text{Information Signal Bandwidth} \times \text{Modulation Index}$$

since this transmission bandwidth provides adequate quality for almost all types of information signals.

The greater the modulation index, the greater the noise and interference immunity of the transmitted signal. The output signal to noise ratio (SNR) of a demodulated FM signal is greater than the RF signal to noise ratio (RF SNR) by a factor related to the modulation index, as described in Chapter 6.

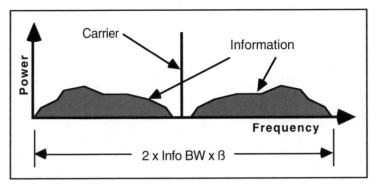

Figure 4-13 FM Signal in Frequency Domain

Single Sideband

Single sideband signals are in effect amplitude modulated signals with the carrier and one sideband filtered off. Although they are more complex to generate and demodulate than AM signals, they occupy about half of the spectrum width. The spectrum occupancy of a single sideband signal equals the information bandwidth, and the RF signal to noise ratio is equal to the demodulated signal to noise ratio.

Modulations for Digital Signals

Before they can be transmitted, digital signals must be amplitude modulated (Figure 4-14), phase modulated (Figure 4-15), or frequency modulated onto an RF carrier.

The simplest frequency modulation scheme is frequency shift keying (FSK) in which one frequency represents a digital zero and another represents a digital one (see Figure 4-16). The frequency spectrum has more than just those two spectral lines, however, because of the sudden frequency change which occurs when the digital signal switches from a zero to a one.

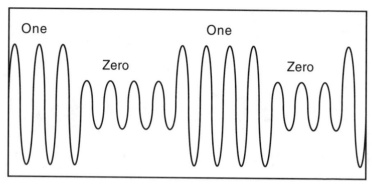

Figure 4-14 Amplitude Modulated Digital Signal

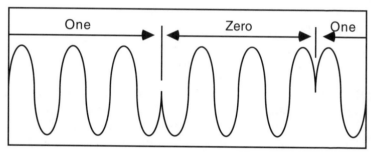

Figure 4-15 Phase Modulated Digital Signal

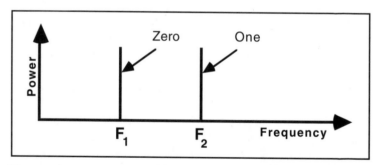

Figure 4-16 FSK Modulated Digital Signal

The RF spectral occupancy of a digital signal depends on two factors: the digitization and the modulation.

Digitization

Analog signals, for example voice or music, are converted to digital form by "digitization." The required number of bits per unit time (the bit rate) is determined by the following factors:

- **The sample rate**, the rate at which the input waveform must be sampled in order to allow accurate reproduction after demodulation. It is usually twice the highest frequency contained in the information signal.

- **The digitization level**, the number of bits per sample, must be great enough to provide adequate signal to quantizing noise ratio.

- **The overhead**, the number of bits that are added to the bit stream to provide synchronization, addresses, parity checks, and error correcting codes, typically varies from 10% to more than 100% of the bits dedicated to the information being transmitted. The highest overhead rates are associated with systems using extensive error detection and correction schemes.

The total bit rate (in bits per second) is:

Bit rate = 2 x Information Bandwidth x sample rate x (1 + overhead factor)

In many applications, the transmitted information is originally digital, for example when one computer communicates with another. In this case, the total bit rate is:

Bit rate = Information Bit rate x (1 + overhead factor)

Communication system specifications are often written in terms of "byte rate" (usually one byte = 8 bits, but not always) or "message rate," (a standard message being some fixed number of bytes). In order to determine the transmission bandwidth required, or to predict the link performance, it is necessary to convert either of these to the equivalent bit rate.

Modulation for Transmission

Various techniques are used to modulate the digital bit stream onto an RF carrier for transmission. Each has advantages and disadvantages which depend on the specific application. When viewed from the perspective of communication link throughput performance, each can be characterized in terms of the amount of RF bandwidth required to transmit a specified bit rate.

Common practice is to filter the RF modulated signal so that 90% of the signal energy is captured by the receiver. For most types of modulations commonly used, this yields a ratio of RF bandwidth (in Hz) to bit rate in bits per second (bps) which varies over the range one to two.

RF Bandwidth typically = 1 to 2 Hz per bps

Table 4-3 shows several popular modulation schemes, along with the RF frequency occupancy factor each requires. This is important information, because digital links are often specified in terms of their digital throughput characteristics. From Table 4-3, you can see that the choice of a frequency-efficient modulation approach dictates an RF bandwidth (in Hz) numerically equal to the bit rate (in bps).

Table 4-3 Bandwidth Factors for Various Modulations
Used for Digital Data

Modulation	Bandwidth Factor (Hz/bps)
Frequency-shift Keying (FSK)	2
Binary Phase-shift Keying (BPSK)	2
Quadriphase-shift Keying (QPSK)	1
Minimum-shift Keying (MSK)	1

This will allow you to use the formulas in Chapters 5 and 6 of this book to predict digital link performance.

4.2.3 Power Amplifier

Modulation normally is done at low power levels, then the power amplifier increases the signal power to the level required to achieve the required transmission range, and outputs a signal to the transmitting antenna. The power amplifier output power can range from few milliwatts to many kilowatts. This power is stated in dBm for link analysis purposes. Since the total radiated power is the transmitter power plus (in dB) the antenna gain, there is a trade-off between transmit antenna gain and transmitter power.

The maximum transmitter output power available depends on the type of power amplifier used, the signal duty cycle, and the frequency range.

Solid state amplifiers are lower in power output and are restricted to lower frequency ranges than various types of tube amplifiers ... but have been significantly more reliable in operation, particularly in rugged environments. However, both of these factors change constantly. A great deal of work is being done to improve tube reliability and both the maximum power and frequency range of solid state amplifiers are constantly being increased.

The duty cycle of the signal makes a significant difference in the maximum output power available. The peak power of a continuous wave (CW) signal is equal to its average power. However, the average power of a pulsed signal can be two or three orders of magnitude less than its peak power.

Although the state of the art is continually changing, CW amplifiers with greater than 1 kilowatt of output have been hard to find for a long time, while pulse amplifiers capable of hundreds of kilowatts have been common for many years.

4.3 Receivers

The receiver performs the following link functions:

• Eliminates all but the desired signal (or signals).

• Demodulates the received signal to reconstruct the original information signal input to the transmitter.

• Band limits the received signal for sensitivity.

Many different types of receivers have been developed to perform these functions, and the techniques vary depending on the frequency range, the type of signals to be received, and other operational considerations. Table 4-4 shows a few of the many types of receivers in common use, along with the characteristics of each. These few types have been chosen for discussion to facilitate later discussions of the impact of the receiver on link performance. The relative merits of different types of receivers are usually described in terms of their selectivity and sensitivity.

Table 4-4 Various Types of Receivers

Receiver Type	Characteristics
Fixed Tuned	Good selectivity & sensitivity Dedicated to one signal
Channelized	Combines selectivity & sensitivity with wide band coverage
Super-Heterodyne	Most common type of receiver Good selectivity & sensitivity
Crystal Video	Wideband instantaneous coverage Low sensitivity and no selectivity Mainly for pulsed signals
IFM	Coverage , sensitivity & selectivity like crystal video Measures frequency of received signals
Digital	Highly flexible Can deal with signals with unknown parameters

Selectivity is the ability to ignore undesired signals or interference, and is typically related to the instantaneous bandwidth covered. Sensitivity defines the weakest signal that can be received. The characteristics described in this table are generalities, useful in the selection of a type of receiver to perform a particular task. However, it must be recognized that the selectivity and sensitivity of an individual receiver of any type can vary over a wide range.

4.3.1 Fixed Tuned Receiver

The fixed tuned receiver (Figure 4-17) typically monitors a single transmitter or an important broadcast frequency. The tuner normally includes a fixed tuned preselection filter to limit the input to the single frequency of interest. The demodulator is appropriate for the signals to be received, and the recovered information signal can either be output to a listener or further processed.

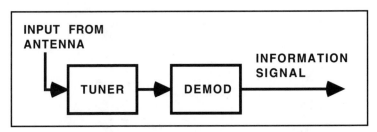

Figure 4-17 Fixed Tuned Receiver

Fixed tuned receivers typically have high sensitivity and good selectivity. They are also usually small, light, reliable, and relatively inexpensive -- all because they have relatively few components. However, they are necessarily lacking in flexibility because they are not tunable.

Examples of practical fixed tuned receivers are single frequency communication receivers, emergency broadcast channel monitors, weather report receivers, and paging receivers. A very interesting application of a fixed tuned receiver is for receipt of global positioning system (GPS) signals. The GPS signals come from many different satellites, four or more of which are usually within view of any receiver. However, each signal contains a different code which uniquely spreads its spectrum. By applying the correct code, the GPS receiver reconstructs an individual signal and effectively tunes out all other signals. The scheme is called code division multiple access (CDMA), and was selected for several reasons, including the practicality of using simple (and economical) fixed tuned receivers.

4.3.2 Channelized Receiver

To monitor large frequency ranges, several fixed tuned receivers can be organized into a channelized receiver as shown in Figure 4-18, to demodulate the whole frequency range with high sensitivity. The filter bank normally divides the frequency range being covered into contiguous channels. (i.e. The filters for adjacent channels have the upper 3 dB frequency of the lower channel equal to the lower 3 dB frequency of the upper channel).

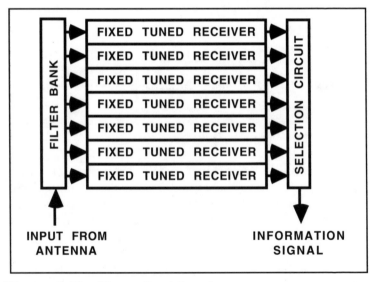

Figure 4-18   Channelized Receiver

The big advantage of a channelized receiver is that it can simultaneously look at and demodulate signals over its full frequency range with high sensitivity and selectivity.

4-20

The output selection circuit can then output any appropriate number of demodulated signals for recording or further processing. The disadvantage of the channelized receiver is its high complexity and cost relative to other types of receivers.

State of the art packaging techniques are making channelized receivers more and more practical. However, channelized receivers remain significantly more complex and expensive than most other types of receivers, so their use is limited to applications which require high probability of receiving large numbers of signals, some of which are simultaneous. The best examples are in the Electronic Warfare field, where receiving many signals in an extremely short time frame is literally a matter of life and death.

As a practical matter, channelized receivers are usually used in combination with switchable band selectors which operate on the superheterodyne principle so that a single channelized receiver with a reasonable number of channels can be quickly assigned where it is needed over a large frequency band.

4.3.3 Superheterodyne Receiver

The superheterodyne (commonly called "superhet") receiver is the most widely used type of receiver. Its great charm is that it can provide virtually any type of performance that is required (within the limits of the laws of physics, of course). It allows infinite tradeoffs of sensitivity and selectivity against band coverage and tuning speed. It can cover relatively wide frequency ranges with relatively low complexity. For these reasons, commercial AM, FM and short wave broadcast receivers are almost universally superhets.

Figure 4-19 shows the basic block diagram of a superhet receiver. This diagram is for a single conversion receiver. Actual superhet receivers often have significantly greater complexity, including two or three frequency conversions to cover all of the required frequency range with acceptable received signal quality. They may also have several selectable IF amplifiers (with different bandwidths) and/or multiple demodulators.

Almost all superhet receivers have tunable "preselection" filters to limit the input frequency range. As you will see in Chapter 6, these filters can negatively affect the sensitivity. Receiver designs in which sensitivity is more important than selectivity may use very wide tunable filters or fixed tuned preselectors for lower loss.

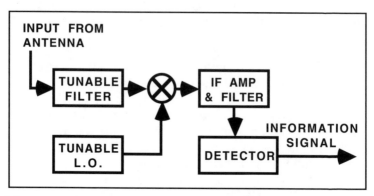

Figure 4-19   Superheterodyne Receiver

A tunable local oscillator (L.O.) allows the receiver to be tuned to different portions of its frequency range. The tuning of the L.O. is offset from the receiver's tuned frequency by a fixed amount. Common offsets are 455 kHz in HF, 10.7 MHz or 21.4 MHz in VHF and UHF, and 21.4 MHz, 60 MHz or 160 MHz in microwave receivers. In modern receivers, the L.O. is usually a synthesizer that tunes rapidly and accurately to any frequency in its range with a single digital control input.

The local oscillator signal and any signals passing through the input filter are both injected into a mixer. The mixer output then contains all of the following signals:

- All input signals from the filter

- The L.O. signal

- The sums and differences of those signals

- All harmonics of all input signals and *their* sums and differences

This mess is passed to an intermediate frequency (IF) amplifier/filter which is at an offset frequency as discussed above (e.g. 21.4 MHz). Since the IF filters are fixed tuned, they can have very sharp cutoffs, eliminating all of the mixing products except a replica of the signal coming through the input filter but centered at the IF frequency. IF filtering also (usually) sets the predetection bandwidth of received signals. The receiver may have several, selectable IF bandwidths. The IF amplifier provides most or all of the gain to bring signals up to the level required for discrimination.

The discriminator (also called detector or demodulator) recovers the modulation from the received signal to reconstruct the original information signal which was input to the transmitter. The type of discriminator used depends on the the type of modulation which has been applied to received signals. Many receivers have multiple, selectable discriminator types (e.g. AM, FM, SSB …).

This superhet approach can also move "chunks" of frequency spectrum around using a switched converter. In a typical application, a set of band pass filters divides a wide input range into even segments, each segment is then "heterodyned" to a single output band using the same approach used in the superheterodyne receiver, but with a switched local oscillator having only one frequency per band. This allows a relatively narrow receiver (for example a 2 to 4 GHz channelized receiver) to cover a much wider frequency range (for example 2 to 12 GHz).

4.3.4 Crystal Video Receiver

The crystal video receiver is an AM (crystal) detector preceded by a band pass filter and (usually) a preamplifier, and followed by a video amplifier. It continuously covers its entire frequency range, AM detecting all signals present.

This means that the crystal video receiver has a 100% probability of detecting any AM signal it sees, but cannot separate multiple overlapping signals. It is also severely limited in sensitivity since the detector operates on low level received signals in what is called the "square law" region. Superhet receivers provide better sensitivity because their detection takes place in the "linear region" after a significant amount of amplification.

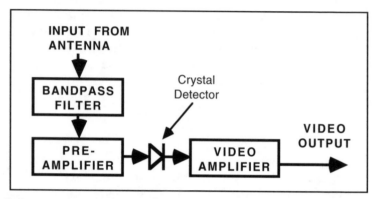

Figure 4-20 Crystal Video Receiver

Crystal video receivers are mainly useful for pulse signals, which have very short duty cycle and in many useful applications reach the receiver at strong signal levels. Although it provides good time of arrival, amplitude and shape information about pulses, the crystal video receiver gives no information about the frequency of received pulses except that they are within the limits of its bandpass filter.

4.3.5 IFM Receiver

Often used as a companion to crystal video receivers, instantaneous frequency measurement (IFM)receivers give very high speed digital measurements of the frequency of received signals. They have approximately the same sensitivity as crystal video receivers, and cover up to octave bandwidths.

Figure 4-21 shows the block diagram of a typical IFM receiver. A hard limiting amplifier is required because the IFM discriminator is highly sensitive to received signal amplitude, and can give accurate frequency measurements only when all input signals are at the same signal strength.

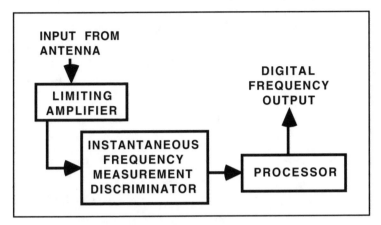

Figure 4-21   IFM Receiver

4.3.6 Digital Receiver

The digital receiver is in some ways the simplest type of receiver -- at least in hardware. A received signal is merely digitized. Then a computer of some type performs all of the demodulation and filtering functions in software. The great advantage of the digital receiver comes in its flexibility. Since filters and demodulators are implemented in software, they can have virtually any parameters, including some that could not be achieved in hardware.

Digitized signals can be stored and sequentially subjected to different filtering and demodulation until the desired output quality is achieved. Stored, digitized frequency bands can be sequentially searched to detect types of signals that cannot even be observed until they have been subjected to some level of processing.

That was the good news. The bad news is that the state of the art in analog to digital converters is not adequate to digitize low level RF signals in very wide bandwidths. Also, when predetection signals are digitized with enough resolution to provide good results, over any significant signal duration, they occupy vast amounts of memory.

Practical digital receivers require some compromises, as shown in Figure 4-22. First, a switchable translator is usually used to select a reasonable portion of RF spectrum to process. Then, a "zero IF" translator is used to heterodyne the undiscriminated band down in frequency until its lower edge is near zero Hz. This brings the whole frequency band within the range of the analog to digital (A/D) converter.

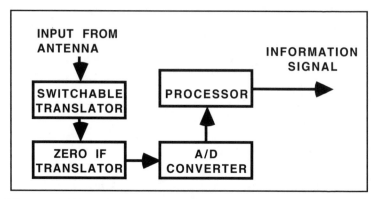

Figure 4-22 Digital Receiver

There are clever tricks (like submultiple sampling) that can be used under some circumstances to simplify or improve this process, but they will not be discussed here. Also, the upper frequency and throughput rate of A/D converters and improved digital storage media are the subject of much serious research and development. Available performance changes almost daily.

Although there are limits to what they can do, digital receivers are already very useful in several important applications, and their applications are constantly expanding with the improvements in component state of the art.

4.3.7 Receiving Systems

Receivers are often organized into receiving systems including preamplifiers, signal distribution networks, and multiple receivers of the same or different types. Figure 4-23 shows a typical receiving system. It is important to note that the performance of each individual receiver in the communication link is significantly impacted by the characteristics of the hardware in the signal path between the antenna and the receiver's input connector. There are often practical reasons to have receivers far separated from the antenna location. If so, the cable losses from the antenna to the preamplifier and from the preamplifier to the receiver(s) can cause significant loss of link performance if the system is not properly designed.

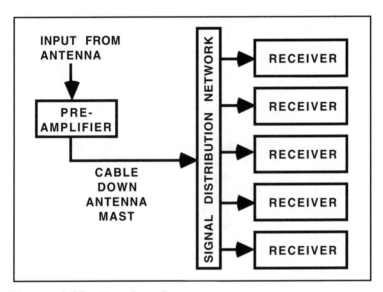

Figure 4-23 Receiver System

Chapter 6 discusses receiver system sensitivity calculation techniques, including the effects of preamplifier specifications, receiver specifications, and system losses before and after the preamplifier.

4.4 Antennas

Antennas convert signal power from the transmitter into electromagnetic waves ... and then convert them back into signal power that can be processed by the receiver. We characterize antennas in terms of their gain and directivity. The gain is the amount that the antenna increases the signal strength of signals which it transmits or receives. Directivity is the quality of providing more gain in one direction than the antenna provides in other directions. These two qualities are interactive, since antenna gain is the result of concentrating a transmitted signal into a limited angular space, or conversely focusing on a limited angular space to concentrate the received signal. At any given angle, the antenna gain can be either positive or negative (in dB). Two other important antenna qualities discussed in this section are efficiency and polarization.

4.4.1 Antenna Gain Pattern

An "isotropic" antenna is a theoretical antenna which would provide exactly equal gain in all (spherical) directions. The gain of such an antenna would be one (1), i.e. zero dB. True isotropic antennas do not exist for two reasons. First, a true isotropic antenna would have to have 100% efficiency (which no antennas built by humans achieve). Second, any real antenna must have a signal cable attached to it and must be mounted somehow, but anything near an antenna distorts its gain pattern.

Still, the isotropic antenna is an important concept. Antenna gain in any direction is typically defined relative to the gain which would be provided by an isotropic antenna. Also, the assumption that an isotropic antenna is placed at some critical point in space allows the development of formulas which greatly simplify propagation calculations.

Figure 4-24 shows a typical antenna gain pattern. This is a polar plot of antenna gain vs. angle like that generated in antenna test chambers (called anechoic chambers because their walls absorb all signal energy reaching them). An antenna is mounted in the center of the

4-28

chamber and rotated through 360° either vertically or horizontally. Signals are transmitted to the antenna, and its output is recorded as a polar plot of received strength, which represents the relative gain of the antenna vs. angle.

As shown in the figure, the "boresight" of the antenna is normally its point of maximum gain. Zero degrees of angle is defined at the boresight, and the signal strength is usually plotted against a logarithmic scale ... so the plot shows dB of gain vs. degrees from boresight. The vertical pattern is called the "elevation" pattern, and the horizontal pattern is called the "azimuth" pattern.

Several other values are shown in this figure. The 1 dB beamwidth (BW) is the angular spread between the two points on either side of the boresight where the antenna gain is 1 dB less than the boresight gain. It is important to note that this is the angle between the two 1 dB points, *not* the angle from the boresight to the 1 dB point. (Lots of people make that mistake.)

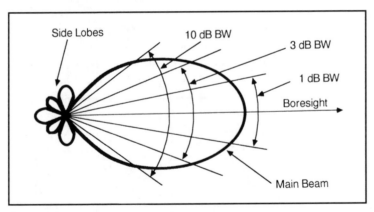

Figure 4-24   Antenna Gain Pattern

The 3 dB beamwidth is the angle between the "half power points" of the antenna beam ... that is the points at which the antenna gain is 3 dB less than the boresight gain. When people talk about "antenna beamwidth"   without defining it with some number of dB, they normally mean the 3 dB beamwidth. The 10 dB beamwidth is, of course, the angle between the -10 dB gain points (relative to boresight gain).

The "main beam" is the primary lobe of the antenna gain pattern … for which the antenna is designed. The "side lobes" (including the "back lobe") are normally treated as undesirable features of the antenna, and defined in terms of their minimum gain difference below the boresight gain. For example, "The sidelobes are 25 dB down."

An important antenna concept is the tradeoff of gain vs. beamwidth, logical since a directional antenna "directionally concentrates" the transmitted power. If there were no side lobes and no losses in the antenna hardware, the antenna would be 100% efficient. The efficiency achieved (always less than 100%) is a function of the type of antenna, the quality of its construction, the way in which it is mounted, and the frequency range it is designed to cover. Efficiency of 55% is common for narrow frequency range antennas. Figure 4-25 is a graph of boresight gain vs. 3 dB beamwidth for a 55% efficient antenna.

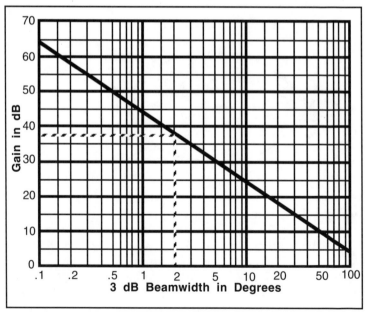

Figure 4-25 Gain vs. Beamwidth

To use this figure, move right from the antenna gain to the line, then down to the 3 dB beamwidth appropriate to that amount of gain, or reverse the procedure to find the gain for a specified beamwidth. The example on the chart shows that a 55% efficient antenna with a 3 dB beamwidth of 2° will have 37.5 dB gain.

Another assumption in Figure 4-25 is that the antenna pattern has the same vertical and horizontal beamwidth. This is not always the case, but the following two convenient equations can be used to determine the approximate boresight gain vs. the 3 dB beamwidth in two mutually perpendicular planes.

The first of these equations is for 55% efficient antennas (a widely assumed value for parabolic dishes):

$$\text{G (not in dB)} = \frac{29,000}{\theta_1 \times \theta_2}$$

Where: θ_1 & θ_2 Are the 3 dB beamwidths measured in any mutually orthogonal planes

Remember that this is *not* the gain in dB. To determine the gain in dB, use the dB conversion technique described in chapter 2 to get:

$$\text{G (dB)} = 10 \ \log \left(\frac{29,000}{\theta_1 \times \theta_2} \right)$$

The same formula for antennas with 60% efficiency (a commonly assumed value for horns) is:

$$\text{G (not in dB)} = \frac{31,000}{\theta_1 \times \theta_2}$$

Where: θ_1 & θ_2 Are the 3 dB beamwidths measured in any mutually orthogonal planes

For Gain in dB, the equation is:

$$G\ (dB) = 10\ \log \left(\frac{31,000}{\theta_1 \times \theta_2} \right)$$

Another important way to describe antennas is in terms of their "effective area." This does not always correspond in any satisfying way with the physical size of the antenna -- although they are related. The effective area can be mathematically defined in terms of the antenna gain and the frequency of the signal being transmitted or received, using the following formula:

$$A = 38.6 + G - 20\ \log\ (F)$$

Where: A = Effective area (in dBsm)
G = Boresight gain (in dB)
F = Frequency (in MHz)

Remember that dBsm is the ratio of the antenna area to one square meter, converted into dB form. It should also be noted that 38.6 (which is often rounded to 39 when 1 dB accuracy is enough) is a combination of various constants and conversion factors to allow the gain to be input in dB and the frequency to be input in MHz. Appendix A includes a derivation of this formula.

Effective antenna area in square meters is found by converting the value for area in dBsm back into "linear" form using the technique described in chapter 2:

$$A\ (m^2) = 10^{\left(\frac{A(dBsm)}{10} \right)}$$

Figure 4-26 is a nomograph (based on the above formulas) which conveniently relates peak antenna gain, effective antenna area and frequency. This figure allows you the flexibility to determine any one factor in this three way relationship in terms of the other two.

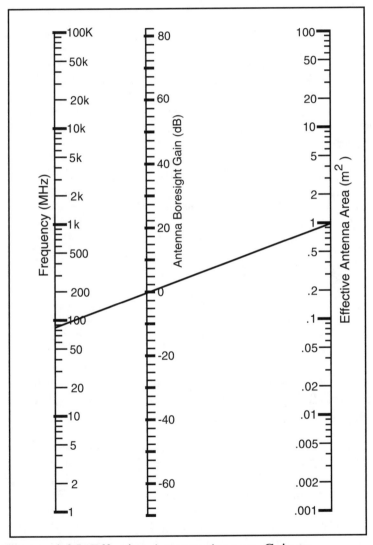

Figure 4-26 Effective Antenna Area vs. Gain vs. Frequency

The example shown on this figure is our old friend the isotropic antenna (which you will remember has unity (i.e. 0 dB) gain. Drawing a line from 1 m^2 on the area line through 0 dB on the gain line shows that an isotropic antenna has an effective area of 1 square meter at approximately 85 MHz.

4.4.2 Polarization

The polarization of an electromagnetic wave refers to the orientation of its electrical and magnetic fields. The critical thing to understand about polarization is that the transmitting and receiving antennas must have the same polarization or an additional "polarization mismatch" loss is experienced by the receiving antenna.

The polarization of the transmitting antenna determines the polarization of the transmitted signal. Most antennas have one of four principle polarizations:

- Vertical (V)

- Horizontal (H)

- Right hand circular (RHC)

- Left hand circular (LHC)

In addition to these four, antennas can be linearly polarized at any angle (45° is fairly common), or can have elliptical polarization (particularly when viewed from an angle off of the boresight).

Polarization, unlike some aspects of communication theory, has a satisfying physical logic to it in most cases. Vertically oriented antennas (for example a common whip antenna) have vertical polarization, while horizontally oriented antennas have horizontal polarization, and most (but not all) circularly polarized antennas are round (for example spirals). Also satisfying is what happens to signals when they reflect from flat surfaces. For example, a vertically polarized signal which reflects from an angled surface will come away with a linear polarization that is no longer vertical.

Figure 4-27 shows the polarization loss for various signal polarizations when they are received by antennas with matched or unmatched polarization

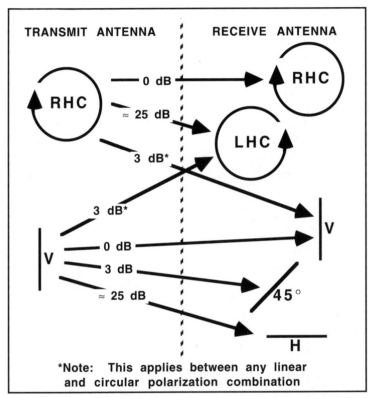

Figure 4-27 Polarization Losses for Antenna Polarization Mismatches

In the real world, received signals often include many multipath components in addition to the primary signal (reflections of the same signal from buildings, trees, the ground, the antenna support structure, etc.) This gives the received signal a cross polarization component, so the actual polarization loss may be less than shown. However, where there is clear line of sight between the transmitting and receiving antennas, the direct signal will usually be much larger than the multipath components, so these loss figures can be considered fairly accurate estimates.

Polarization loss is not always bad. For example, a receiving system could be designed with a right hand circularly polarized antenna to significantly reduce interference from a strong left hand circularly polarized signal at the same frequency as the desired signal. This is often done in systems to send control signals from Earth stations to satellites.

A circularly polarized antenna is often used in the design of systems to receive many different linearly polarized signals which can be vertical, horizontal, or anything in between. The uniform 3 dB polarization loss is experienced for all received signals, but that is preferable to the much greater loss that would be experienced for cross polarized signals.

4.4.3   Types of Antennas

Table 4-5 is a summary of the most common types of antennas. For each type, it shows the general gain pattern and *typical* specifications. It is important to understand that individual antennas can be designed to meet a range of gain, bandwidth, and beamwidth parameters around the typical values listed, and that these parameters trade off against each other. Each antenna type can be used as either a transmitting or receiving antenna, and will have the same specifications and general configuration. However, the construction of high power transmitting antennas is somewhat different to handle the increased currents.

Because they are more conceptually complex, the last two antenna types in the table (dishes and phased arrays) are described in more detail following the table.

Table 4-5   Types of antennas

Antenna Type	Pattern	Typical Specifications
Dipole	El ∞ Az ◯	Polarization: Vertical Beamwidth: 80° x 360° Gain: 2 dB Bandwidth: 10 % Frequency Range: zero through μw
Whip	El ⌒⌒ Az ◯	Polarization: Vertical Beamwidth: 45° x 360° Gain: 0 dB Bandwidth: 10 % Frequency Range: HF through UHF
Loop	El ∞ Az ◯	Polarization: Horizontal Beamwidth: 80° x 360° Gain: -2 dB Bandwidth: 10 % Frequency Range: HF through UHF
Normal Mode Helix	El ⌒⌒ Az ◯	Polarization: Horizontal Beamwidth: 45° x 360° Gain: 0 dB Bandwidth: 10 % Frequency Range: HF through UHF
Axial Mode Helix	Az & El	Polarization: Circular Beamwidth: 50° x 50° Gain: 10 dB Bandwidth: 70 % Frequency Range: UHF through low μw
Biconical	El ∞ Az ◯	Polarization: Vertical Beamwidth: 20° to 100° x 360° Gain: 0 to 4 dB Bandwidth: 4 to 1 Frequency Range: UHF through mmw

Table 4-5 Types of Antennas (Continued)

Antenna Type	Pattern		Typical Specifications
Lindenblad	El		Polarization: Circular Beamwidth: 80° x 360° Gain: -1 dB Bandwidth: 2 to 1 Frequency Range: UHF through µw
	Az		
Swastika	El		Polarization: Horizontal Beamwidth: 80° x 360° Gain: -1 dB Bandwidth: 2 to 1 Frequency Range: UHF through µw
	Az		
Yagi	El		Polarization: Horizontal Beamwidth: 90° x 50° Gain: 5 to 15 dB Bandwidth: 5% Frequency Range: VHF through UHF
	Az		

Log Periodic	El		Polarization:
			    Vertical or Horizontal
			Beamwidth: 80° x 60°
			Gain: 6 to 8 dB
			Bandwidth: 10 to 1
			Frequency Range:
			    HF through µw

	Az		
Cavity Backed Spiral	El & Az		Polarization: R & L Circular Beamwidth: 60° x 60° Gain: -15 dB (min freq) +3 dB (max freq) Bandwidth: 9 to 1 Frequency Range: µw
Conical Spiral	El & Az		Polarization: Circular Beamwidth: 60° x 60° Gain: 5 to 8 dB Bandwidth: 4 to 1 Frequency Range: UHF through µw

Table 4-5 Types of Antennas (Continued)

Antenna Type	Pattern	Typical Specifications
4 Arm Conical Spiral	El Az	Polarization: Circular Beamwidth: 50° x 360° Gain: 0dB Bandwidth: 4 to 1 Frequency Range: UHF through μw
Horn	El Az	Polarization: Linear Beamwidth: 40° x 40° Gain: 5 to 10dB Bandwidth: 4 to 1 Frequency Range: VHF through mmw
Horn with Polarizer	El Az	Polarization: Circular Beamwidth: 40° x 40° Gain: 5 to 10dB Bandwidth: 3 to 1 Frequency Range: μw

Parabolic Dish
 	
 Feed
	El & Az	Polarization:
		          Depends on Feed
		 Beamwidth: 0.5 to 30°
		 Gain: 10 to 55dB
		 Bandwidth:
		          Depends on Feed
		 Frequency Range:
		          UHF to μw

Phased Array
 	
 Elements
	El
	 Az
		Polarization:
		          Depends on Elements
		 Beamwidth: 0.5 to 30°
		 Gain: 10 to 40dB
		 Bandwidth:
		          Depends on Elements
		 Frequency Range:
		          VHF to μw

Parabolic Dish Antennas

Parabolic dish antennas (commonly called just "dishes") are parabolic reflectors which reflect signals from a feed antenna located at the focus of the parabola as shown in Figure 4-28. The feed antenna is normally a horn, log periodic or spiral antenna. Dish antennas have a great deal of flexibility in application because their gain and beamwidth are dependent on their size and the operating frequency, while their polarization and bandwidth are set by the feed.

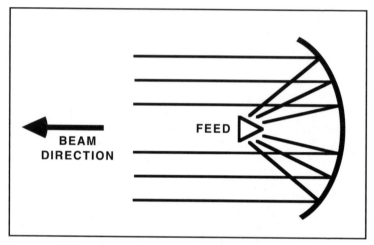

Figure 4-28 Parabolic Dish Antenna Concept

The relationship between the gain of a parabolic reflector antenna (with 55% efficiency), its diameter, and the operating frequency can be calculated from:

$$G = -42.2 + 20 \log(D) + 20 \log(F)$$

Where: G = Antenna gain (in dB)
D = Reflector diameter (in meters)
F = Frequency (in MHz)

-42.2 combines several constants and conversion factors (see Appendix A) to allow input of diameter and frequency in these units.

Figure 4-29 is a nomograph (based on the above equation) of gain vs. size vs. frequency for 55% efficient parabolic dish antennas. In the example, a one half meter diameter antenna operating at 10 GHz is shown to have approximately 32 dB of gain. Only relatively narrow frequency range antennas (about 10% bandwidth) achieve 55% efficiency. Wider frequency coverage by an antenna will reduce its efficiency.

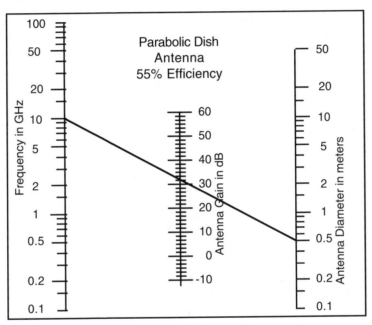

Figure 4-29   Parabolic Dish Antenna Gain vs. Diameter vs. Frequency

Table 4-6 shows the gain adjustments necessary to compensate for antenna efficiency factors other than 55%. To use this table, find the antenna gain from Figure 4-29, then adjust the gain by adding or subtracting the number of dB indicated in the table.

A few antenna manufacturers make excellent paper slide-rules that allow you to quickly determine the gain and beam width of antennas of any reasonable size, with any efficiency, operating at any frequency. They also provide

Table 4-6 Gain Adjustments vs. Efficiency

Antenna Efficiency	Adjustment to Gain in Figure 4-29
60%	Add 0.4 dB
50%	Subtract 0.4 dB
45%	Subtract 0.9 dB
40%	Subtract 1.4 dB
35%	Subtract 2 dB
30%	Subtract 2.6 dB

several other important values (like the 10 dB beam width, the angle from the boresight to the first side lobe, etc.)   The marketing department of any company which has the slide rules will normally send you one free if you write an official looking letter of request. However, one company gave me official permission to tell you exactly how to get their "Antenna Calculation Slide Rule." Write or call:

Tecom Industries, Marketing Department
9324 Topanga Canyon Blvd
Chatsworth, CA 91311-5795
(818)341-4010 (Ask for Marketing)

Just ask for the slide rule by name and tell them where to send it. They said they will send one, at no charge, to anyone who knows enough about antennas to ask.

Phased Array Antennas

A "phased array antenna" is an array of several simple antennas connected to a transmitter or receiver through variable delay lines as shown in Figure 4-30. This drawing is for a receiving antenna, but would work the same for a transmitting antenna. The delay lines are adjusted so that the signals from the antennas add in-phase (maximizing the combined signal power) when the signal arrives from the "beam direction." This causes an effective gain in the desired direction. Signals arriving from other directions add out-of-phase, which significantly decreases the combined signal power.

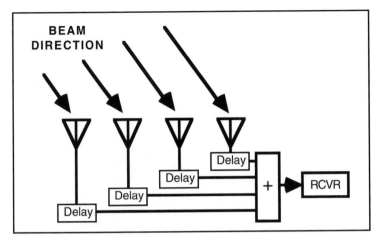

Figure 4-30 Phased Array Concept

If electrically controlled delay lines are used, the phased array beam is said to be "electronically steered." This gives it the great advantage over any other type of directional antenna that it can be instantly moved to any pointing angle without the delays caused by rotating a mechanical antenna structure.

Phased arrays can be constructed using any type of antennas, but usually use simple dipoles or flat spiral antennas which can be built into a flat surface (etched or deposited) with great precision. This gives them very low relative thickness, a great advantage for some applications (for example mounting on an aircraft). In high power transmitting phased arrays, horn antennas are often used. They can be built into a single structure which allows the use of very thin material for applications in which weight is a significant problem.

The length of a phased array and the operating frequency determine the beam width. For example a 3 dB beam width of 3 degrees requires an array 20 wave lengths long. (i.e. At 6 GHz it must be 20 x 5 cm or 1 meter long.) The spacing of the antennas in the array determine the angular range over which the antenna can be steered without degrading the antenna performance below the specified value. A good typical number for the efficiency of a relatively narrow bandwidth phased array is 30%.

Table 4-7 is an antenna selection guide to assist in the selection of antenna type from the various specifications required by an application.

4.5 The "Ether Waves"

The rest of the communication link is what happens between the transmitting and receiving antennas as the signals pass through the atmosphere (or space) between them. The simplest case is when the two antennas have clear line of sight. In this case, the signal strength is only reduced by spreading loss and atmospheric attenuation -- which are discussed in Chapter 5. When the two antennas do not have line of sight or when signals must pass through rain or fog, the communication link will still function, but there will be additional losses as described in Chapter 7.

Table 4-7 Antenna Selection Guide

Angular Coverage	Polar- ization	Band Width	Antenna Type
360° Azimuth	Linear	Narrow	Whip, Dipole, or Loop
		Wide	Biconical or Swastika
	Circular	Narrow	Normal Mode Helix
		Wide	Lindenblad or 4 Arm Conical Spiral
Directional	Linear	Narrow	Yagi, Array with Dipole Elements or Dish with Horn Feed
		Wide	Log Periodic, Horn or Dish with Log Periodic Feed
	Circular	Narrow	Axial Mode Helix or Horn with Polarizer or Dish with Crossed Dipole Feed
		Wide	Cavity Backed Spiral, Conical Spiral or Dish with Spiral Feed

Chapter 5

THE LINK EQUATION

The *link equation* described in this chapter calculates received signal power as a function of the various link parameters described in Chapter 4. It is also sometimes called the "one way link equation" to distinguish it from radar equations that deal with round trip propagation.

It is a little misleading to talk about the link equation as though it were a single equation -- there are actually several equations that are used to answer the real-world questions you want answered:

• How much transmitter power is required to transmit over a given range?

• How much receiver sensitivity is required to adequately receive a given signal at a given range?

• How much antenna gain (transmit and/or receive) is required?

• What is the effective range of a transmitter with a particular output power?

Like most real-world problems, the answer to each of these questions is "That depends!" Each of these questions is readily answered by use of different forms of the "link equation" with applicable values plugged in.

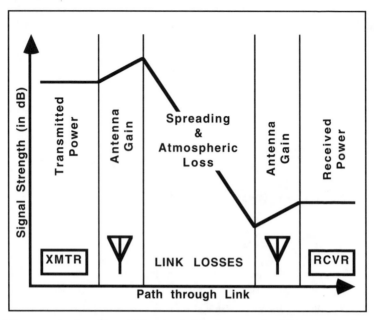

Figure 5-1   Signal Strength Variations through the Link

Figure 5-1 shows an overview of what happens to a signal as it progresses through the communication link. The signal:

- Originates in a transmitter which outputs a "transmitted power" level.

- Is radiated by an antenna which provides gain.

- Is reduced in signal strength by link losses.

- Is received by an antenna which provides gain.

- And arrives at a receiver with a "received power" level.

The whole purpose of the "link equation" is to calculate the signal strength arriving at the receiver, given all of the other factors. Thus, in its simplest form (with all values in dB forms), the link equation is:

```
        Transmitter Power

    +  Transmitting Antenna Gain

    -  Link Losses

    +  Receiving Antenna Gain
    _____

    =  Received Power
```

The most commonly used units are:

- Transmitted Power in dBm
- Link losses in dB
- Antenna gains in dB
- Received Power in dBm

Remember that the antenna gain (in dB) can be either positive or negative, and is also a function of the angle at which the signals arrive or leave (i.e. relative antenna orientation). The gain used in this equation (for both transmitting and receiving antennas) is the gain in the direction of the other antenna -- whether or not the boresights of the antennas are aligned to each other. Throughout this book, *losses* are considered to be positive numbers -- so they can be *subtracted* in the various link equation forms.

Example

Transmitter Power = 10 Watts (= +40 dBm)

Transmitting Antenna Gain = 6 dB

Link Losses = 100 dB

Receiving Antenna Gain = -2 dB

_____

Signal strength received by the receiver = -56 dBm

More about using this equation to solve those practical

problems after discussing the causes and calculation of link losses.

5.1   Link Losses

In this chapter, we assume a "line of sight" link in good weather. There are no obstructions between the two antennas (including the curvature of the Earth) and the signal path stays a wavelength or two away from the surface. (Chapter 7 will discuss messier link situations, and show how to calculate their effects.)

There are two types of losses in a line of sight link:

> • Spreading Loss -- which is a function of frequency and distance (between isotropic antennas)

> • Atmospheric Loss -- which is a function of frequency and distance through the atmosphere

5.1.1 Spreading Loss

Spreading loss is caused by the dispersion of signal energy as it radiates away from the transmitting antenna.

From a perfect "isotropic" antenna radio waves would spread out spherically ... like someone was blowing up a balloon. To continue the analogy, the balloon gets thinner as it expands -- because the same amount of rubber is distributed over the expanding surface area of the sphere. The transmitted signal energy is likewise distributed over an expanding spherical surface.

Leaving the analogy before the balloon pops, the total signal energy remains the same at any distance from the transmitter, but is distributed over the surface of a huge sphere of radius equal to that distance. The surface area of that sphere is $4\pi d^2$.   If we had a receiving antenna that could capture the whole sphere, there would be no spreading loss. However, any practical antenna will capture only a small part of the sphere as shown (in two dimensions) in Figure 5-2. The effective antenna area (discussed in Section

4.4.1) and the radius of the sphere (i.e. the distance from the transmitter) determine the fraction of the sphere's surface captured by the antenna.

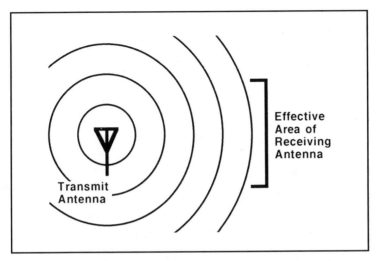

Figure 5-2 Transmitted Wavefront and Receiving Antenna Area

In the formula for spreading loss presented here, it is assumed that both the transmitting and receiving antennas are *isotropic* (with 0 dB gain). This is a great convenience, since it allows us to add the gains (in dB) of the transmitting and receiving antennas as separate numbers when determining received signal strength.

From the ratio of the surface area of the expanding sphere and the effective area of an isotropic receiving antenna (which varies with frequency) we get a well behaved formula for the spreading loss between two isotropic antennas:

Spreading Loss = A Constant x frequency^2 x distance^2

In dB form, this equation becomes:

$$L_S = K + 20 \log(F) + 20 \log(d)$$

The constant (K) is another of those contrived numbers which include several constants and unit conversion factors to allow convenient input and output units. If you input the distance in kilometers and the frequency in MHz, the constant will be 32.44 (commonly rounded to 32 for 1 dB accurate calculations). The spreading loss is then defined by:

$$L_S = 32 + 20 \log(F) + 20 \log(d)$$

Where: L_S = Spreading loss in dB
F = Frequency in MHz
d = Distance in km

We will be using this formula often in the later parts of this chapter. For your convenience, this same equation is presented in Appendix E for distance in statute or nautical miles; the only difference is that each has a different constant. The formula is derived in Appendix A.

It is important not to fall in love with the expanding balloon analogy, which only literally applies if there is a truly isotropic transmitting antenna. The same formula applies equally well for transmission between any two antennas which have unobstructed line of sight to each other. The L_S equation tells what the loss would have been if both *were* truly isotropic, which allows the antenna gains to be added separately in link equations.

When a dB or two of accuracy is plenty, you may find it more convenient to use the spreading loss nomograph shown in Figure 5-3. Draw a line from the frequency (in GHz) on the left hand scale to the distance (in km) on the right hand scale. The spreading loss in dB is the point at which the line crosses the center scale. In the example shown on the nomograph, the spreading loss for a 1 GHz signal at 20 km is about 118 dB. (Remember that the constant in the L_S equation above was rounded down from 32.44 to 32.) This same nomograph is presented for distance in statute or nautical miles in Appendix E at the end of the book.

5-6

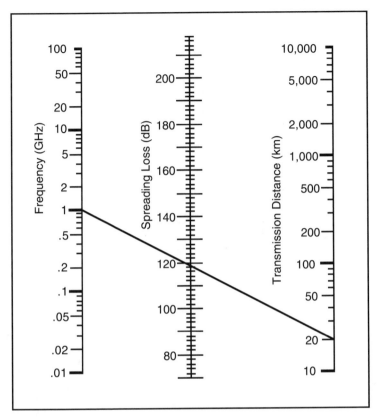

Figure 5-3 Spreading Loss Nomograph

5.1.2 Atmospheric Loss

Atmospheric loss is caused by the absorption of radio energy (mainly by oxygen and water vapor) as signals pass through the earth's atmosphere. The combined losses per kilometer are shown as a function of frequency in Figure 5-4. Note that this curve is for attenuation horizontally through the troposphere near the earth's surface.

To use this chart, enter at the transmission frequency along the bottom of the chart, move straight up to the curve, and read the loss per unit distance on the left scale. Assuming that the whole transmission path is in the atmosphere, the total atmospheric loss is the loss per unit distance multiplied by the link distance. For example, at 45 GHz, the atmospheric loss is about .4 dB per kilometer, so a 10 km link at 45 GHz would have 4 dB of atmospheric loss.

Notice that there is a very strong peak in atmospheric attenuation at about 58 GHz, which would make this a very poor choice for an earth transmission link, but excellent for transmitting from satellite to satellite if you didn't want anyone on the earth to listen in.

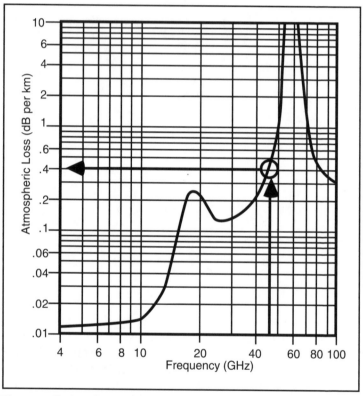

Figure 5-4 Combined Atmospheric Loss per Kilometer

Another thing to notice about this chart is that the atmospheric attenuation gets very small at low frequencies. Below microwave frequencies, it is usually acceptable to ignore the atmospheric attenuation as negligible, particularly when making calculations to 1 dB accuracy.

Equivalent curves are given in Appendix E for atmospheric attenuation per statute mile and nautical mile.

Figure 5-5 shows a family of curves for the atmospheric attenuation through the Earth's whole atmosphere for satellite to ground links, as a function of frequency and the elevation angle of the satellite above the horizon at the ground station. There is naturally much higher attenuation at low elevation angles because much more of the transmission path is within the atmosphere.

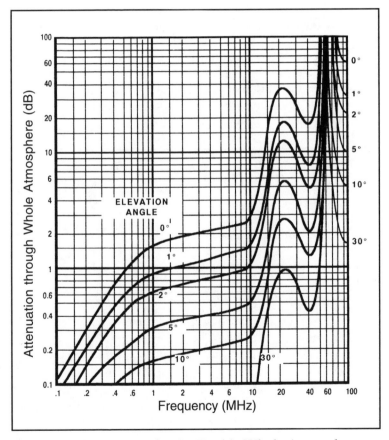

Figure 5-5 Attenuation by Earth's Whole Atmosphere

5.2 Signal Strength at Various Points in the Communication Link

In the design or evaluation of a communication link, it is necessary to pin down the signal strength at various points in terms of the link variables (transmitter power, antenna gains, and link losses). This section deals with the link points commonly considered. In each case, an equation for the signal strength at that point in the link will be given in terms of the other defined signal strengths, gains and losses in the link.

5.2.1 Effective Radiated Power

The effective radiated power (ERP) is the signal power radiated from the transmitting antenna in the direction of the receiving antenna. It is typically expressed in dBm. It is the sum of the transmitter power (in dBm) and the applicable antenna gain (in dB).

$$ERP = P_T + G_T$$

Where:

P_T = Transmitter Power (dBm)

G_T = Transmit Antenna Gain (dB)

As shown in Figure 5-6, the ERP is very much a function of the link geometry. Assuming a transmitter power of 10 Watts (+40 dBm): if the receiver is at point A, the ERP is + 50 dBm; if it is at point B, the ERP is only +41 dBm. However, *if someone talks about ERP without mentioning the geometry, he or she means the ERP at the peak gain of the antenna* .

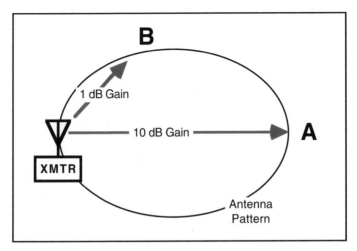

Figure 5-6 Effective Radiated Power

Defining ERP in dBm is very useful, and will give accurate results. However, it must be noted that we are taking some literary license in describing ERP in power units (dBm), since it is actually out in the "ether waves" between the two antennas. In fact, the signal travels between the two antennas in the form of an electromagnetic wave which is more accurately defined in terms of its electrical field density (in microvolts per meter). Power (in milliwatts or dBm) is technically only defined inside a circuit.

The artifice used is to describe the electromagnetic wave's field density in terms of the power that would be produced at the output of an isotropic (i.e. unity gain) antenna placed at the point we are considering. This approach immensely simplifies the book keeping, and is accurate enough for all but the most hard-core technical types.

In the case of ERP, this imaginary isotropic antenna would be placed right at the antenna, so close that there would be no link loss (but ignoring the effects of being in the antenna's "near field," which would distort the results).

In case you need to express ERP in field density units, you can convert back and forth between microvolts per meter (μv/m) and dBm using the following formulas (which are derived in Appendix B):

To convert from μv/m to dBm

$$P = -77 + 20 \log(E) - 20 \log(F)$$

Where: P = signal strength in dBm
E = Field strength in μv/m
F = Frequency in MHz

To convert from dBm to μv/m

$$E = 10^{\left(\frac{P + 77 + 20 \log(F)}{20}\right)}$$

5.2.2 Signal Arriving at Antenna

The strength of signals arriving at the antenna (P_A) is a useful consideration because it is often necessary to evaluate tradeoffs of different types of antennas. It can also be important to determine the effect of an antenna gain pattern in the rejection of interfering signals.

The magnitude of the signal arriving at the receiving antenna is the effective radiated power (ERP) in the direction of the receiving antenna reduced by all link losses. This includes the spreading loss and the atmospheric loss for line of sight links in good weather, but will also include the losses described in Chapter 7 for more challenging propagation situations.

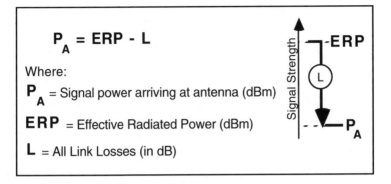

$$P_A = ERP - L$$

Where:

P_A = Signal power arriving at antenna (dBm)

ERP = Effective Radiated Power (dBm)

L = All Link Losses (in dB)

The link losses (for good weather, line of sight links) include spreading loss and atmospheric loss.

$$L = L_s + L_{Atm}$$

Where: L_s = Spreading loss

L_{Atm} = Atmospheric Loss

This can be combined with the expression for spreading loss given in Section 5.1.1 to make the very useful formula shown below.

For Good Weather, Line of Sight Links

$$P_A = ERP - 32 - 20 \log(F)$$
$$- 20 \log(d) - L_{Atm}$$

Where: P_A = Signal strength at receiving antenna (dBm)

ERP = Effective Radiated Power (dBm)

F = Frequency (MHz)

d = distance (km)

L_{Atm} = Atmospheric loss (dB)

For example, if the signal frequency is 100 MHz, the ERP is +50 dBm and the receiver is 50 km from the transmitter with clear line of sight and good weather, the signal power arriving at the receiving antenna would be:

+50dBm	- 32dB	- 20 log(100)dB	- 20 log(50)dB
= +50dBm	- 32dB	- 20(2)dB	- 20(1.7)dB
= +50dBm	- 32dB - 40dB	- 34dB	= -56dBm

Note that atmospheric attenuation is negligible at 100 MHz

Like ERP, the signal strength arriving at the receiving antenna can be easily converted from dBm to μv/m using the formulas given in Section 5.2.1 above. This may be quite useful, since the sensitivity of some types of receiving systems with integral antennas (for example direction finding systems) is sometimes specified as field strength in μv/m.

5.2.3 Received Power

You will notice that "received power" is the answer in the link equation as defined at the beginning of this chapter. It is the signal power input to the receiver from the receiving antenna, and is equal to the signal strength arriving at the antenna plus the effective receiving antenna gain.

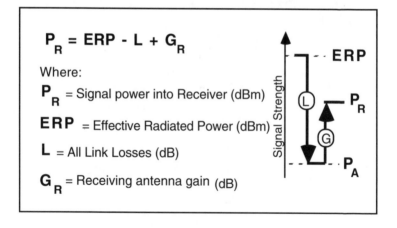

$$P_R = ERP - L + G_R$$

Where:

P_R = Signal power into Receiver (dBm)

ERP = Effective Radiated Power (dBm)

L = All Link Losses (dB)

G_R = Receiving antenna gain (dB)

It is normally assumed that the receiving antenna gain value is its peak gain, but this is not *always* the case. For example, when an interfering signal is received from a direction away from the intended transmitter, its received power is calculated using the antenna gain in the direction of the interfering transmitter. Another important case is when a narrow beam receiving antenna cannot be perfectly aligned. In this case, the G_R value used may be the gain at the maximum anticipated misalignment angle.

There are often significant cable runs between the receiving antenna and the receiver, and there may also be preamplifiers involved, so there is an important "book-keeping" issue here. You need to be very clear about exactly where the received power is defined. In this book, it will always be defined at the output of the receiving antenna, since that is the point at which the antenna's gain is defined. This means that any preamplifiers and/or cable runs are considered part of the receiver (or receiving system)

When the above equation for received signal power is combined with the expression for spreading loss given in Section 5.1.1 it yields:

For Good Weather Line of Sight Links

$$P_R = ERP - 32 - 20 \log(F)$$
$$- 20 \log(d) - L_{Atm} + G_R$$

Where: P_R = Signal strength into receiver in dBm
   ERP = Effective Radiated Power in dBm
   F = Frequency in MHz
   d = distance in km
   L_{Atm} = Atmospheric loss in dB
   G_R = Receiving antenna gain in dB

For example, if the signal frequency is 100 MHz (so L_{Atm} is negligible), the ERP is +50 dBm, the receiver is 50 km from the transmitter within line of sight, and the receiving antenna gain is 3 dB (in the direction toward the transmitter) the received power would be:

$$+50dBm \quad - 32dB \quad - 20\log(100)dB - 20\log(50)dB + 3dB$$
$$= \ +50dBm \quad - 32dB \quad - 20(2)dB \qquad - 20(1.7)dB \quad + 3dB$$
$$= \ +50dBm \quad - 32dB - 40dB \qquad - 34dB \qquad + 3dB$$
$$= -53dBm$$

5.3 Link Design Parameters

This section describes several important link design parameters in terms of the link variables which control them and the signal levels to which they relate.

5.3.1 Required Margin

Because it is an imperfect world, things go wrong ... particularly in radio communication links. It might rain, antennas may not stay perfectly aligned, there may be fading caused by reflections of our desired signal (from stationary or moving objects), or there may be unexpected external sources of noise or interference. To make the link dependable, more than the minimum acceptable signal level must be provided for the receiver.

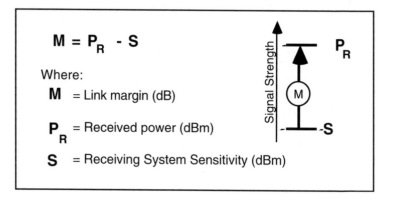

The minimum signal level that a receiver can receive and still do its job is called its sensitivity. Sensitivity is a signal power level and is usually expressed in dBm. (You will learn to calculate the sensitivity in Chapter 6.) The amount by which the received power level exceeds the sensitivity is called the link margin. Margin is expressed in dB, and can be achieved either by increasing the arriving signal strength or by improving the sensitivity. The tools available for providing margin depend on what parts of the link and the link geometry are under your control. They could include:

- Increasing the transmitter power

- Increasing the transmitting antenna gain

- Increasing the receiving antenna gain

- Decreasing the operating range

- Improving the receiver sensitivity

The amount of margin required depends on the link's operating situation and on how important it is that the link be reliable. A general rule of thumb is that you should provide a margin equal to the inverse of the average drop-out time ratio you can tolerate ... converted to dB. Examples are:

- For 10% link drop-out time, provide 10 dB margin
  ($1/0.1 = 10$ $10 \log(10) = 10$ dB)

- For 1% link drop-out time provide 20 dB margin
  ($1/0.01 = 100$ $10 \log(100) = 20$ dB)

- For 0.1% link drop-out time provide 30 dB margin
  ($1/0.001 = 1000$ $10 \log(1000) = 30$ dB)

5.3.2 Required Sensitivity

The sensitivity of a receiver is a specification of the minimum signal strength it can receive and still reproduce the transmitted information signal with adequate quality.

If you must provide a receiving system to receive signals from an existing transmitter, at some specified range, the only variables you have to work with are the receiving antenna gain and the receiver sensitivity. Assuming for a moment that you must also work with an existing receiving antenna, you can calculate the *required receiver sensitivity* as follows:

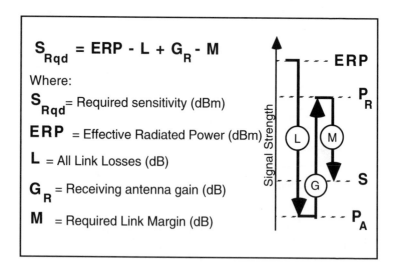

$$S_{Rqd} = ERP - L + G_R - M$$

Where:

S_{Rqd} = Required sensitivity (dBm)

ERP = Effective Radiated Power (dBm)

L = All Link Losses (dB)

G_R = Receiving antenna gain (dB)

M = Required Link Margin (dB)

Again, this can be combined with the expression for spreading loss given in Section 5.1.1 to make the very useful formula shown below.

For Good Weather Line of Sight Links

$$S_{Rqd} = ERP - 32 - 20 \log(F) - 20 \log(d) - L_{Atm} + G_R - M$$

Where: S_{Rqd} = Required Sensitivity in dBm

ERP = Effective Radiated Power in dBm

F = Operating Frequency in MHz

d = Distance from Transmitter in km

L_{Atm} = Atmospheric Loss in dB

G_R = Receiving Antenna Gain in dB

M = Required Link Margin in dB

For example, if the signal frequency is 100 MHz (so L_{Atm} is negligible), the ERP is +50 dBm, the receiver is 50 km from the transmitter within line of sight, the receiving antenna gain is 3 dB (in the direction toward the transmitter), and you must have 20 dB of performance margin -- the required receiver sensitivity (in dBm) would be:

$$+50\text{dBm} - 32\text{dB} \quad - 20\log(100)\text{dB} \quad - 20\log(50)\text{dB} + 3\text{dB} - 20\text{dB}$$
$$= +50\text{dBm} - 32\text{dB} \quad - 20(2)\text{dB} \qquad\qquad - 20(1.7)\text{dB} \quad + 3\text{dB} - 20\text{dB}$$
$$= +50\text{dBm} - 32\text{dB} \quad - 40\text{dB} \qquad\qquad - 34\text{dB} \qquad\quad + 3\text{dB} \quad - 20\text{dB}$$
$$= \underline{-73\text{ dBm}}$$

5.3.3 Effective Range

The effective range of a communication link is the maximum distance between the transmitting and receiving antennas for which the link can still do its job. You will often read an advertisement for a transmitter or a receiver with "a range of five miles." This may or may not be true, depending on a number of assumptions. Accurately specifying effective range requires the specification of every element of the link.

The only effect that operating range has on a line of sight link is the amount of link loss it causes. Thus, the *effective range* is the transmitter to receiver distance at which the maximum *acceptable* link loss occurs. This makes the received signal equal to the receiver sensitivity plus the required margin. The total link loss is customarily considered in two parts -- spreading loss and atmospheric loss.

$$L = L_S + L_{Atm}$$

Both are dependent on the operating range. Figure 5-4 shows atmospheric loss *per kilometer* (through the atmosphere). It is a non-linear function that does not readily lend itself to mathematical characterization. Spreading loss, however, is a well behaved function of the expression presented in Section 5.1.1.

Since the atmospheric loss is insignificant at lower frequencies, and is significantly less than the spreading loss for almost all links, the normal approach to determining effective range is to:

1. Determine the acceptable total link loss.

2. Estimate the approximate atmospheric loss to a dB or so and subtract this amount from the total link loss (at UHF and below the estimate is typically zero).

3. Calculate the range at which the spreading loss equals the remaining loss. This is the effective range.

4. Check the atmospheric loss at that calculated range. If it is significantly different from the original atmospheric loss estimate, go back to step 2 with the new estimate and calculate a new effective range.

Yes, you can also set up an equation with the two types of losses vs. range and solve for range, but it's an ugly equation because the atmospheric loss varies with the range and a non-calculatable function of frequency, while the spreading loss varies with range and frequency squared. Almost nobody does it that way unless they have a lot of calculations to do and can run them on a computer.

The heart of the process is step 3 above, which starts with the spreading loss expression from Section 5.1.1:

$$L_S = 32 + 20 \log(F) + 20 \log(d)$$

Where: L_S = the spreading loss in dB
F = the operating frequency in MHz
d = the transmitter to receiver distance in km

This expression can be rearranged into:

$$20 \log(d) = L_S - 32 - 20 \log(F)$$

from which the distance can be determined as:

$$d_{(in\ km)} = 10^{\left(\frac{L_S - 32 - 20 \log F}{20}\right)}$$

Now, the trick is to determine the allowable (spreading) link loss and plug it into that formula. The allowable loss is the difference between the ERP and the signal strength arriving at the antenna (P_A) minus the atmospheric attenuation. But for the receiver to properly reproduce the information signal, the input signal to the receiver (P_R) must at least equal the receiver's sensitivity level (S). If we require a margin (M), P_R must be above S(dBm) by M(dB). Therefore, the received power must reach the receiver with a signal strength of at least S + M (dBm). Since the receiving antenna adds G_R dB of gain, P_A must be at least S + M - G_R (dB). So the maximum acceptable spreading loss is defined by the following expression:

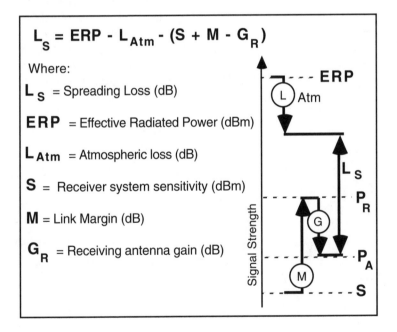

$$L_S = ERP - L_{Atm} - (S + M - G_R)$$

Where:

L_S = Spreading Loss (dB)

ERP = Effective Radiated Power (dBm)

L_{Atm} = Atmospheric loss (dB)

S = Receiver system sensitivity (dBm)

M = Link Margin (dB)

G_R = Receiving antenna gain (dB)

When the expression for d has this expression for L_S plugged in, it gets really cumbersome, so let's create a new variable "20 log(d)" for convenience. This is in fact the dB representation of the square of the range from the transmitter to the receiver, and is defined by the following expression:

$$20 \log (d) = ERP - S + G_R - L_{Atm} - M$$
$$- 32 - 20 \log(F)$$

Now the range (the transmitter to receiver distance) is defined by the expression:

$$d_{(in\ km)} = 10^{\left(\frac{20\ \log(d)}{20}\right)}$$

Which is the way you will probably want to calculate it anyway.

For example, if the signal frequency is 100 MHz (meaning that there is negligible atmospheric loss), the transmitter ERP is +50 dBm (in the direction toward the receiver), the receiver sensitivity is -73 dBm, the receiving antenna gain is +3 dB (in the direction toward the transmitter), and you must have 20 dB of performance margin the effective link range (in kilometers) would be calculated as follows:

$$20 \log(d) = ERP - S + G_R - L_{Atm} - M \quad - 32 - 20 \log(F)$$

$$[20 \log (F) = 20 \log(100)dB = 40\ dB]$$

$$20 \log(d) = +50dBm + 73dBm + 3dB - 0dB \quad - 20dB - 32dB - 40dB$$
$$= \underline{34dB}$$

Note that the sensitivity is a negative number (so becomes positive in the expression) and that the atmospheric attenuation is negligible at 100 MHz. So the effective range of the link is calculated from "20 log(d)" as:

$$d_{(in\ km)} = 10^{\left(\frac{34}{20}\right)} = 10^{1.7} = 50\ km$$

5.3.4 Required Transmitter Power or Antenna Gain

It is a straightforward process to determine the required transmitter power or the gain required of either the transmitting or receiving antenna if the other link parameters are established. If all elements are expressed in dB or dBm: The transmitter power and the transmitting antenna gain sum to the effective radiated power (ERP). The ERP is then reduced by the link loss to the signal level at the receiving antenna. The receiving antenna gain is subtracted from the receiver sensitivity to determine the minimum level that the signal strength at the receiving antenna can be for proper link operation. However, to provide link margin, the signal strength at the receiver must be greater than that minimum by M dB. In an equation this is:

$$P_T + G_T - L = S - G_R + M$$

Where: P_T = Transmitter Power (dBm)

G_T = Transmitting Antenna Gain (dB)

L = Combined Link Losses (dB)

S = Receiver Sensitivity (dBm)

G_R = Receiving Antenna Gain (dB)

M = Link Margin (dB)

Each of the following three formulas is a reorganization of the above formula to solve for one of the six values in terms of the other five. The assumption in each case is that five of the six values are set because the hardware exists, the link geometry is required, or that value has been calculated earlier.

Required Transmitter Power:

$$P_T = S - G_R + M + L - G_T$$

For example, if the receiver sensitivity is -80 dBm, a 20 dB margin is required, the total link losses (spreading + atmospheric) are 110 dB, the transmitting antenna has 10 dB gain, and the receiving antenna has 3 dB gain -- adequate link performance requires the transmitter power to be:

$$-80\text{dBm} - 3\text{dB} + 20\text{dB} + 110\text{dB} - 10\text{dB} = \underline{+\ 37\ \text{dBm}}$$
(Which is 5 watts)

Required Transmitting Antenna Gain:

$$G_T = S - G_R + M + L - P_T$$

For example, if the receiver sensitivity is -80 dBm, a 20 dB margin is required, the total link losses are 110 dB, the transmitter power is 10 watts (+40 dBm), and the receiving antenna has 3 dB gain -- adequate link performance requires the transmitting antenna gain to be:

$$-80\text{dBm} - 3\text{dB} + 20\text{dB} + 110\text{dB} - 40\text{dBm} = \underline{7\ \text{dB}}$$

Required Receiving Antenna Gain:

$$G_R = S - P_T - G_T + M + L$$

For example, if the receiver sensitivity is -80 dBm, a 20 dB margin is required, the total link losses (spreading + atmospheric) are 110 dB, the transmitter power is 1 watt (+30 dBm), and the transmitting antenna has 10 dB gain -- adequate link performance requires the receiving antenna gain to be:

$$-80\text{dBm} - 30\text{dBm} - 10\text{dB} + 20\text{dB} + 110\text{dB} = \underline{10\ \text{dB}}$$

5.4   Interfering Signals

Whether considering unintentional interference or deliberate jamming, the following discussion will allow you to determine the ratio of a radiated interfering signal to the desired signal -- as "seen" by the receiver.

It is important to understand that it is only what the receiver "sees" (as signals entering through its input connector) that matters. If the interfering transmitter is at a location different from that of the transmitter producing the desired signal, the receiving antenna pattern may cause a difference in the antenna gain for the desired and interfering signals. Also, if the interfering signal is not at the exact same RF frequency as the desired signal, its interference may be attenuated by filtering anywhere in the receiving system.

For the rest of Section 5.4, we will use the following assumptions:

- The receiver tuning is centered on the desired signal.

- The receiving antenna boresight is pointed at the desired signal's direction of arrival.

- The interfering transmitter is located remote from the transmitter generating the desired signal so that its range and angle of arrival are different.

The physical arrangement is then as shown in Figure 5-7.

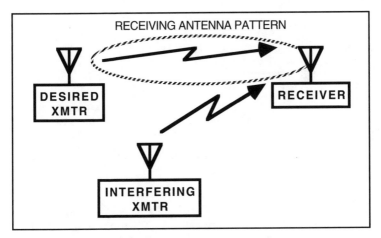

Figure 5-7 Interference Geometry

The definition of three new terms will help us deal with interfering signals:

I/S = Interference to Signal Ratio = the power ratio of the interfering signal to the desired signal at the receiver input, but only as the receiver can receive it.

I_A = Angular Isolation = the boresight gain of the receiving antenna - the gain of the receiving antenna in the direction of the interfering transmitter.

I_F = Frequency Isolation = the amount of attenuation that all of the filters in the receiving system apply to the interfering signal, relative to the throughput of the desired signal.

I_F is a little tricky because "frequency isolation" can have several causes as shown in Figure 5-8. If the interfering signal is within the frequency range of desired signals, but not at the frequency of the *specific* desired signal, it is generally attenuated only by filters within the receiver. If outside the frequency range of desired signals, it may be further attenuated by a bandpass filter before the receiver. If it is outside the frequency range of the receiving antenna, the antenna will act like a filter, providing additional attenuation.

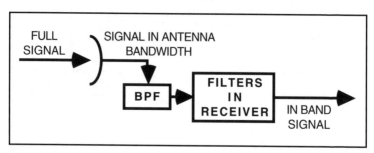

Figure 5-8 Filtering Isolation

In general, it is the *ratio* of an interfering signal to the desired signal (I/S) that causes trouble, since automatic or manual gain control in a receiver can generally take care of problems associated with the absolute power of interfering signals received. The I/S ratio is calculated from:

$$I/S = ERP_I - ERP_S - L_I + L_S - I_A - I_F$$

Where: I/S = Interference to signal ratio (dB)
ERP_I = the ERP of the interfering signal (dBm)
ERP_S = the ERP of the desired signal (dBm)
L_I = the link losses of the interfering signal (dB)
L_S = the link losses of the desired signal (dB)
I_A = the antenna isolation (dB)
I_F = the filter isolation (dB)

By defining "d_I" as the range to the interfering transmitter and "d_S" as the range to the desired signal transmitter, L_I and L_S become: $L_I = 32 + 20 \log(F_I) + 20 \log(d_I)$
$L_S = 32 + 20 \log(F_S) + 20 \log(d_S)$

Assuming negligible difference in atmospheric attenuation between the two signal paths yields the expression:

$$I/S = ERP_I - ERP_S - 32 - 20 \log(F_I)$$
$$- 20 \log(d_I) + 32 + 20 \log(F_S)$$
$$+ 20 \log(d_S) - I_A - I_F$$

which can be simplified in a number of interesting ways.

If the interfering signal is very close in frequency to the desired signal, the two 20 log(F) terms can cancel each other with much less than 1 dB of inaccuracy. If the two signals are *exactly* the same frequency, there will be no filtering isolation, so the I_F term goes out. So, for "in band" interfering signals, the interference to signal ratio is:

For In-band Interference

$$I/S = ERP_I - ERP_S - 20 \log(d_I)$$
$$+ 20 \log(d_S) - I_A$$

Out of band interference is a little more complicated. You need to have some information about the "ultimate rejection" of filters, and need to look at the receiving system configuration to determine which filters will let the interfering signal through and which will attenuate it. When a receiver is installed physically near a very powerful out of band transmitter, a band stop filter is sometimes added specifically to bring the interference to signal ratio within acceptable bounds. Antennas are well specified as to the frequencies they *accept*, but generally make very poor filters, because they are not easily designed to *reject* frequencies. The formula for out of band interference to signal ratio is:

For Out-of-band Interference

$$I/S = ERP_I - ERP_S - 20 \log(d_I)$$
$$+ 20 \log(d_S) - 20 \log (F_I)$$
$$+ 20 \log(F_S) - I_A - I_F$$

The signal environment shown in Figure 5-9 will be used for interference to signal calculation examples. The desired signal is a mobile communications radio with:

ERP = +30 dBm (toward our receiver)
Frequency = 225 MHz
Range = 40 km

Signal I_1 is from a transmitter identical to that producing the desired signal, but 100 km from us. Its transmitting antenna provides an ERP of +30 dBm toward our receiver. Signal I_2 is from a high power commercial broadcast station operating at 100 MHz only 2 km from our receiver. It has ERP = +80 dBm toward our receiver.

First, calculate the I/S ratio for the interfering signal I_1. This is an in-band interfering signal, so the equation is:

$$I/S = ERP_I - ERP_S - 20 \log(d_I) + 20 \log(d_S) - I_A$$

I_A is the difference between the receiving antenna's boresight gain and its gain in the direction of the interfering signal
$I_A = 10 \text{ dB} - 2 \text{ dB} = 8 \text{ dB}$

5-28

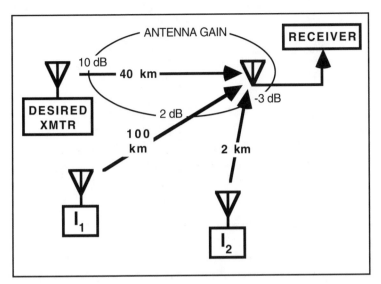

Figure 5-9 Interference Environment

$$
\begin{aligned}
I/S &= 30\text{dBm} - 30\text{dBm} - 20\log(100)\text{dB} + 20\log(40)\text{dB} - 8\text{dB} \\
&= 30\text{dBm} - 30\text{dBm} - 40\text{dB} \qquad\qquad + 32\text{dB} \qquad\quad - 8\text{dB} \\
&= -16\text{dB}
\end{aligned}
$$

The interfering signal is received 16 dB below the desired signal by the receiver -- independent of the frequency of operation. Depending on the modulation, it might be noticeable, but will not prevent proper reception of the desired signal.

Now consider the I/S ratio for interfering signal I_2. This is an out-of-band interference signal, so the equation is:
$$I/S = ERP_I - ERP_S - 20\log(d_I) + 20\log(d_S)$$
$$- 20\log(F_I) + 20\log(F_S) - I_A - I_F$$

I_A is 10 dB - (-3 dB) = 13 dB. I_F is not well defined for this example, so lets use some typical numbers. The interfering signal is well out of band, so the ultimate filter rejections will probably be about 60 dB. The type of antenna was not specified, but will probably not give more than 10 dB of frequency rejection, so the total I_F is 70 dB.

$$
\begin{aligned}
\text{I/S} &= +80\text{dBm} \quad -30\text{dBm} \quad -20\log(2)\text{dB} \quad +20\log(40)\text{dB} \\
&\quad -20\log(100)\text{dB} +20\log(225)\text{dB} \quad -13\text{dB} \quad -70\text{dB} \\
&= 80\text{dBm} \quad -30\text{dBm} \quad -6\text{dB} \quad\quad +32\text{dB} \\
&\quad -40\text{dB} \quad\quad\quad +47\text{dB} \quad\quad\quad -13\text{dB} \quad -70\text{dB} \\
&= \underline{0\ \text{dB}}
\end{aligned}
$$

This strong out of band interference signal will be equal to our desired signal, which will probably preclude proper reception. If we can't move away from the interfering signal (a few kilometers would make a big difference), we should look into an extra high pass or band stop filter to reduce the I/S ratio.

5.5 Dynamic Range

Dynamic range is the difference (in dB) between the strongest and weakest signals a receiver or receiving system can accept without degrading its performance. With manual or automatic gain control, a receiver's *total dynamic range* will allow it to accept a very wide range of signal power. This is no problem as long as the desired signal is the strongest (or nearly the strongest) signal that will be received. However, if the receiver must accept a much weaker signal in the presence of stronger in-band signals, its *instantaneous dynamic range* becomes important.

The instantaneous dynamic range is the difference (in dB) between the strongest and weakest signals that can be present in a receiver's passband while the receiver is meeting its full specified performance in receiving and processing the weaker signal.

Whether the total or instantaneous dynamic range definition is used, the maximum strength (in dBm) at which a receiving system can receive and process a signal is the system sensitivity plus the dynamic range. For example, if a receiving system sensitivity is -90 dBm and its dynamic range is 60 dB, the strongest signal it can accept is:

-90 dBm + 60 dB = -30 dBm

Chapter 6

RECEIVER SENSITIVITY

The sensitivity of a receiver defines the weakest signal it can receive and still provide an output of adequate quality. Sensitivity specifications are most commonly stated in dBm, and are usually negative numbers because the sensitivity is almost always less than 1 milliwatt.

An important issue is *where* to define sensitivity. To accurately predict link performance, all of the gains and losses in the receiving part of the link must be counted. Therefore, system sensitivity is usually defined at the output of the antenna as shown in Figure 6-1.

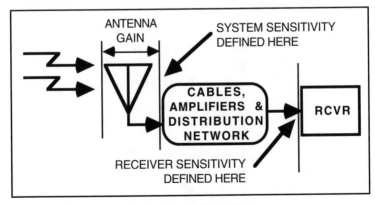

Figure 6-1 Sensitivity Definition Point

It is the *system* sensitivity that has been used in the link equation formulas in Chapter 5. This is important, because when the antenna gain (in dB) is subtracted from the system sensitivity (in dBm), we should get the signal strength which must arrive at the antenna to allow the link to work properly.

If, for some reason, you want to define the system sensitivity at some other point (for example at the end of a cable from the antenna) you can certainly do so, but you'll need to account for the cable loss as a reduction in the antenna gain if you want to use the Chapter 5 formulas.

As you will see later, the first element in the system which provides gain has a dramatic effect on the sensitivity, so you should always define the system sensitivity before the first amplifier when evaluating link performance.

The sensitivity of any receiver or receiver system is determined by the sum of three numbers. They are:

- Thermal Noise Level (kTB)
- Noise figure
- Required signal to noise ratio.

When defining sensitivity in dBm, the sensitivity is related to these three numbers as shown in Figure 6-2.

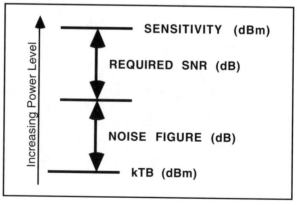

Figure 6-2   Components of Sensitivity

Since numbers expressed in dB are logarithmic, the ratio of signal to noise (in dB) is found by subtracting the noise level (in dBm) from the signal level (in dBm). Since the sensitivity in dBm is normally a negative number, a bigger (i.e. more negative) number equals a smaller signal. (Lots of very smart people get in trouble over that one.)

kTB is the basic thermal noise level in the receiver. It is a function of the operating temperature and the bandwidth.

The *noise figure* is the amount of noise that the receiver system adds.

The *required SNR* (signal to noise ratio) is a function of the output signal quality required. It is the SNR at the system sensitivity definition point (i.e. the output of the antenna) that must be used in calculating sensitivity, and as you will see in Section 6.3 this can be quite different from the output signal SNR for some types of modulation.

It is important to be sure that all three of these components of sensitivity are referenced to the same point in the system ... the point at which you are defining the sensitivity.

6.1   kTB

kTB defines the thermal noise present in an ideal receiver -- the lowest noise that can be theoretically achieved. It is a function of the effective receiver bandwidth and the operating temperature. ("k" is Boltzman's constant, "T" is the system operating temperature, and B is the system bandwidth.)

A commonly used number for kTB is "-114 dBm per MHz" ... which is the thermal noise level for a receiver with a 1 MHz bandwidth operating at standard room temperature (defined as 290°K which is about 63° F or 17°C). Appendix A includes the derivation of this number in case you get a serious case of "urge for rigorousness."

kTB is not very sensitive to temperature changes. The operating temperature has to rise to 92°C (which =198°F and is almost the boiling point of water) to increase kTB by 1 dB. However, it is very sensitive to receiver bandwidth ... varying by 90 dB over the commonly used range of bandwidths. You can calculate kTB at room temperature using the following formula:

kTB = -114 dBm
+ 10 log(Receiver Bandwidth / 1 MHz)

or you could just read it from the chart in Figure 6-3.

To adjust kTB for operating temperature, use the equation:

kTB = Room Temp kTB
+ 10 log(Temp. in °K / 290)

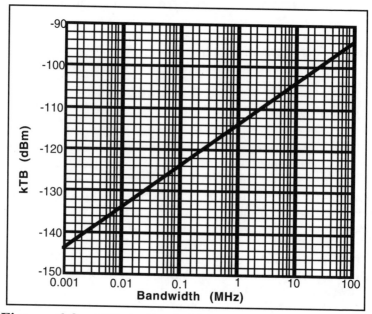

Figure 6-3 kTB vs. Bandwidth

6.2   Noise Figure

The second element of sensitivity is noise figure (NF). It defines the amount of noise the receiver or receiving system adds to received signals (above kTB). System noise figure is a number (typically between 3 and 18 dB) which is derived from the noise figures of the system's amplifiers and receivers and system losses.

The noise figure of an amplifier or a receiver is specified by the manufacturer (in dB). It is determined by measuring the noise level output by the device, but is referenced to the input of the device. Thus, the noise figure is the amount of additional noise that would be input to a perfect, noiseless device to produce the measured level of output noise.

An amplifier's noise figure is its output noise in excess of kTB reduced by the gain. A receiver's noise figure includes the effects of all receiver processing, but is still the amount of noise in excess of kTB which would have to be added at the receiver input to cause its output noise level if the receiver were noiseless.

Receiver System Noise Figure

The noise figure which is summed with kTB and SNR in the sensitivity calculation is the "system noise figure." This is the amount of noise that every element of the system adds, but all referenced to the point at which sensitivity is defined (typically at the antenna output).

The system noise figure is very much a function of the system configuration. The simplest case is shown in Figure 6-4. Here we have a receiver attached to an antenna by a cable, and perhaps passing though some switches, power dividers, or other passive devices. Passive means than they have no gain or other non-linear throughput characteristics. (Switches are OK because they are linear when they are not switching). In this case, the system noise figure is the sum of the receiver noise figure (in dB) and all losses (in dB) between the antenna and the receiver input.

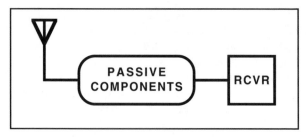

Figure 6-4   Simple Receiving System

System NF = Passive Losses + Receiver NF

For example, if a receiver with 8 dB noise figure is attached to an antenna by a long cable that has 5 dB of loss, the system noise figure is 13 dB.

For more complex systems involving a preamplifier, the system noise figure can be determined from the graph in Figure 6-5. To use this graph, add the preamplifier gain and noise figure, then subtract the losses before the receiver. Run a horizontal line through this value on the left side of the graph. Then run a vertical line through the receiver noise figure at the bottom of the graph. The intersection of these two lines defines the system noise figure degradation from everything down stream of the preamplifier. The system noise figure is then calculated as:

System NF = Loss before Preamp
+ Preamp NF + Degradation

The system configuration for the example drawn on Figure 6-5 is shown in Figure 6-6. The preamplifier noise figure is 5 dB, the preamplifier gain is 20 dB, and the loss before the receiver is 8 dB   (20 + 5 - 8 = 17 dB).   The receiver noise figure is 12 dB.   The two lines cross on the 1 dB degradation line. This means that the system noise figure will be 8 dB. (2 dB of loss before the preamplifier + 5 dB preamplifier noise figure + 1 dB degradation)

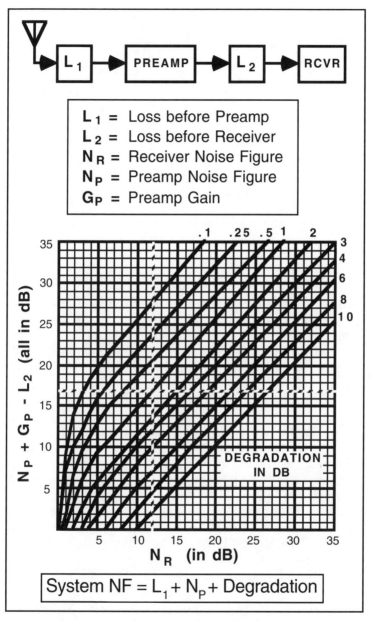

Figure 6-5 Noise Figure in Cascaded Stages

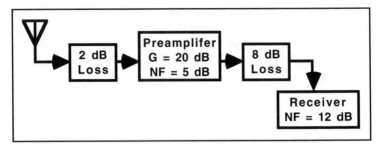

Figure 6-6 Receiver System for Example in Figure 6-5

The main reason for using preamplifiers is that loss before the preamplifier directly reduces the sensitivity, while loss after the preamplifier only degrades sensitivity by a (usually much smaller) degradation factor.

For more complex systems, with more than one preamplifier, start at the receiver and work back toward the front end. First determine the system noise figure at the input of the last preamplifier using the above procedure. Then repeat the procedure using the system noise figure at this point as the "receiver noise figure" while determining the system noise figure looking into the next earlier preamplifier.

6.3 Required Signal to Noise Ratio

The hardest part of defining the sensitivity, at least the part over which the loudest arguments take place, is the definition of "adequate quality." The problem is that "adequacy" depends upon the use to which the information passed by the link is to be put. To be useful in sensitivity definition, "adequacy" must first be reduced to a signal to noise ratio number for the information signal output by the receiver. Then it must be converted to a signal to noise ratio at the antenna output (which is the sensitivity definition point). To differentiate these two signal to noise ratio values (which can be quite different) we will call the signal to noise ratio at the sensitivity definition point the "RF SNR." (Some text books call it the carrier to noise ratio or CNR.)

Table 6-1 shows typical required output SNR values for various types of signals, and the equivalent RF SNR for the modulations indicated. It must be emphasized that this table just gives typical values. The actual output signal to noise ratio required will depend on the specific application. For example, laboratory studies have shown that 16 dB is adequate video signal to noise ratio for trained operators to quickly determine which of several shapes appear on the screen; selection accuracy does not improve with more SNR. But at 16 dB, the picture has so much "snow" that you would probably do violence to a commercial television set with that signal quality.

Table 6-1 Typical Required SNR for Various Signals

Type of Signal	Output SNR	RF SNR
Amplitude Modulated Signals		
Voice Communications	12 dB	12 dB
High Quality AM Radio	30 dB	30 dB
High Quality TV Broadcast	40 dB	40 dB
Pulse Signal (Automatic Processing)	15 dB	15 dB
Frequency Modulated Signals		
Voice Communications	12 dB	12 dB
High Quality FM Radio	30 dB	12 dB
High Quality TV Broadcast	40 dB	12 dB
System using PLL Discriminator	20 dB	4 dB
Digitally Encoded Signals	Depends on Quantizing	12 dB

The following sections will allow you to calculate the RF SNR from the output SNR (and vice versa) for your specific application with the applicable modulation.

6.3.1 Required SNR for AM and Narrow Band FM Signals

Neither amplitude modulation nor narrowband frequency modulation provides any improvement in output SNR relative to the RF SNR (as explained in Section 4.2.2). Therefore, the two SNR figures are identical for these modulations.

6.3.2 Required SNR for FM Signals

Frequency modulation gives performance advantages by spreading the transmitted signal over a frequency band that is wider than the bandwidth of the information signal. The ratio of the transmission bandwidth to the information bandwidth is called the modulation index (ß). The signal to noise ratio of the information signal output from the receiver can be greater than the RF SNR by a factor that is a function of ß. However, to get this improvement factor, the RF signal to noise ratio must be above a threshold factor which depends on the type of FM discriminator used. For the most common type of discriminator, the threshold is about 12 dB, while a phase locked loop (PLL) discriminator will provide the improvement above an RF SNR threshold level of about 4 dB. Providing that the threshold level is met, the signal to noise improvement factor (IF_{FM}) is given by the formula:

$$IF_{FM} = 5 + 20 \log(\text{ß})$$

(For RF SNR > Threshold)

For example, if the modulation index is 5, the improvement factor is:

$$IF_{FM} = 5 + 20 \log(5) = 5 + 14 = 19 \text{ dB}$$

So if the receiver has a normal FM discriminator, a signal with a modulation index of 5 which is received with a 12 dB RF SNR will produce an output signal with SNR = 31 dB.

6.3.3 Required SNR for Digital Signals

Digitized signals are different from analog information signals in that the output "signal to noise ratio" is a function of the way the signal was digitized. The "noise" is not really noise, but distortion caused by the quantizing steps in the digitizing process. This "quantizing noise" is so called because it looks and sounds much like noise to operators. RF noise causes the receiver to generate bad bits, or "bit errors." Bit errors do distort the output information signal, but digital systems are usually specified directly in terms of the bit error rate, since many such systems carry information which has never been in analog form.

Digitized Analog Signals

Figure 6-7 shows an analog signal which is digitized, and what it looks like when it is reconstructed. This figure, and the following discussion assume that pulse code modulation (PCM) is used. This is the most common of several digitization techniques which can provide application specific advantages, but all provide approximately the same throughput quality for the same bit rate.

The two primary considerations in PCM digitization are the number of quantizing levels and the sampling rate.

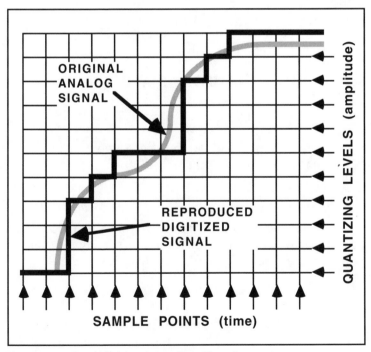

Figure 6-7 Digitized Analog Signal

Sampling Rate

The sampling rate must be at least twice the *highest* information signal frequency to be reproduced. For a simple sine wave, two samples per cycle are enough. A low-pass filter will smooth those two samples per cycle in the output to a perfect sine wave. However, if the curve varies from sinusoidal shape (as the curve in Figure 6-7 definitely does) there are higher frequency components present. The point is that the sampling rate must be high enough to capture any character of the curve that you want to reproduce.

Quantizing Levels

Assuming that there is an adequate sampling rate, the number of digitizing bits per sample determines the signal to quantizing ratio. The number of quantizing levels is 2^m where m is the number of bits per sample, and the signal to quantizing noise ratio (SQR) is given by the following formula, which rounds to 1 dB:

$$\textsf{SQR (in dB) = 5 + 3(2m-1)}$$

Where m = the number of bits per sample

For example, with six bits per sample, the signal to quantizing noise ratio (SQR) is:

SQR = 5 + 3(11) = 38 dB

Table 6-2 shows the number of quantizing levels and the SQR (in dB) for each number of bits per sample up to the limit of common analog to digital converters.

RF Signal to Noise Ratio

The effect of the RF signal to noise ratio is that the noise causes bit errors. The modulator in the transmitter has converted the digital signal (which is a series of "ones" and "zeros") into some sort of modulation medium as described in section 4.2.2. A demodulator in the receiver will convert

6-12

Table 6-2   Quantizing & SNR vs. Bits per Sample

Bits / Sample	Quantizing Levels	Equivalent SNR (in dB)
1	2	8
2	4	14
3	8	20
4	16	26
5	32	32
6	64	38
7	128	44
8	256	50
9	512	56
10	1024	62
11	2048	68
12	4096	74

the received modulation back into a digital bit stream, but the addition of noise to the signal adds uncertainty as shown in Figure 6-8. This figure shows a normally distributed probability density for the modulation value that the signal plus noise could have. For example, if the digital information were carried on a frequency shift keyed modulation, the abscissa would be frequency, the dark arrows represent the one and zero signal frequencies, and the bell shaped curves the probability that a one or zero signal (along with noise) would be at each frequency. The error zones (i.e. a one detected as a zero and a zero detected as a one) are shaded.

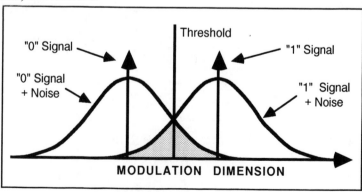

Figure 6-8   Digital Signals + Noise

Although the bit error rate vs. SNR depends on the specific RF modulation used, Figure 6-9 shows the bit error rate vs. RF signal to noise ratio for two types of modulation which span the values of most common modulations. One point of interest is that on the lower part of the curve (where most digital systems are designed to operate) the slope of the lines is about 1 dB per order of magnitude of bit error rate. To pick an example from the chart, a non-coherent FSK modulated digital signal with 11 dB RF signal to noise ratio would achieve a little less than 10^{-3} bit error rate.

The bit error rate is sometimes plotted against E_B/N_O. (E_B is the product of signal power and bit period.) E_B/N_O is not actually a signal to noise ratio, but it determines the RF SNR that would be achieved if the signal were passed through an optimum matched filter for the modulation chosen.

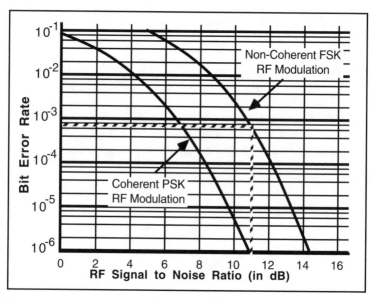

Figure 6-9   Bit Error Rate vs. RF SNR

Chapter 7

CHALLENGING CONDITIONS

This chapter covers some of the challenging conditions we deliberately ignored in the first six chapters. Two of the conditions described (transmission through rain or fog and non-line of sight transmission) add link loss. Each will be described in terms of the amount of loss (in dB) it adds. The third condition described, Doppler shift, causes the received frequency to change with relative motion between the transmitter and receiver.

7.1   Rain and Fog Attenuation

Radio signals are attenuated as they pass through rain and fog -- in excess of the normally accepted atmospheric attenuation levels described in Chapter 5. The bad news is that the charts for rain attenuation given in different references disagree with each other by a dB or so. The good news is that for practical purposes, the absolute numbers are not nearly as important as an understanding of what is going on and the relative rain losses among various alternative link designs.

Anyone who has ever been out in the rain knows that the density of rainfall in any one location changes from minute to minute and a few yards away may be much greater or less. Therefore we need to establish a reasonable rainfall

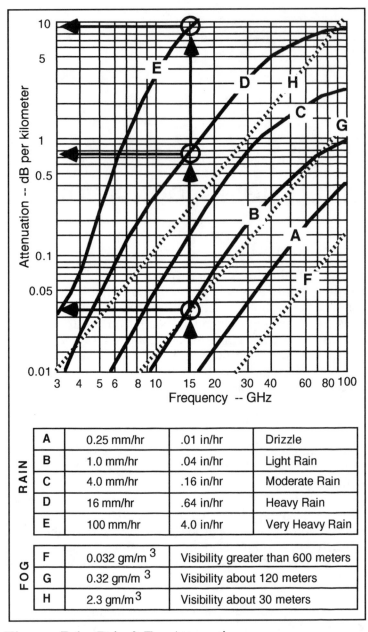

Figure 7-1   Rain & Fog Attenuation

model and determine the amount of attenuation this fixed model causes different link alternatives if we are to compare their performance in bad weather. It is also good practice to use the same model to determine how much link margin to allow in order to assure dependable link operation in bad weather.

Figure 7-1 shows the amount of additional attenuation per unit distance (in kilometers) that is caused by various densities of rainfall and fog. This chart is representative of several found in various references. In Appendix E, you will find equivalent charts for attenuation per statute mile and per nautical mile for your convenience.

To use the chart in Figure 7-1, enter it from the bottom at the link operating frequency, go up to the line corresponding to the rainfall or fog density, then go left to the attenuation per kilometer. The additional attenuation is this number multiplied by the path length (in kilometers) over which the link is subject to that rain or fog density.

The example shown on Figure 7-1 is for a 15 GHz radio link passing through rainfall as shown in Figure 7-2. Notice that the total transmission path length is 50 km. It passes through 10 km of heavy rain and 40 km of light rain.

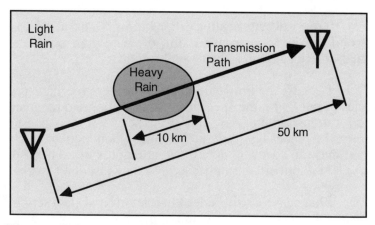

Figure 7-2   Rainfall Model

From Figure 7-1, you can see that the rain attenuation at 15 GHz is 0.035 dB per kilometer for light rain and 0.75 dB per kilometer for heavy rain, so the total rain attenuation for the transmission path in Figure 7-2 is:

$$
\begin{array}{ll}
40 \text{ km x } 0.035 \text{ dB/km} & = 1.4 \text{ dB} \\
10 \text{ km x } 0.75 \text{ dB/km} & = 7.5 \text{ dB} \\
\text{Total Attenuation} & = 8.9 \text{ dB}
\end{array}
$$

Note that Line E on Figure 7-1 shows that 10 km through a typhoon would cause 90 dB of attenuation at 15 GHz.

7.2 Non-line-of-sight Transmission

Up to now, we have assumed that line-of-sight conditions existed -- that is, the transmitting and receiving antennas can "see" each other. But in fact, transmission can take place without direct line of sight in several different ways depending on the frequency of transmission and the operating range.

At Very-Low, Low and Medium frequencies, below 3 MHz, extremely long range propagation by ground wave is common. At High Frequencies, transmissions are reflected from the ionosphere, causing "hops" which can propagate clear around the Earth given the proper conditions.

Tropospheric Scatter propagation is also used for beyond the horizon transmission of very high powered signals, particularly in military applications.

Because the propagation by all of these mechanisms varies greatly with the specifics of transmitter and receiver site locations, time of day, and/or the height of ionospheric layers, the reader is referred to the many handbooks which cover these in adequate detail. No attempt is made here to provide "simplified" formulas because they just don't work.

That leaves knife edge diffraction and diffraction over a spherical surface, which apply in a wide range of practical applications, and for which reasonably accurate nomographs exist. The author has used them in field tests and found the measured results to be reasonably consistent with their predictions.

Knife Edge Diffraction

Knife edge diffraction is the propagation of radio waves over a perfectly absorbing knife edge -- an extreme case of non-line of sight propagation causing significantly greater losses than would be experienced when transmitting over the horizon on a perfectly smooth planet. In practice, this model is a very practical (but conservative) way to characterize what happens as a moving transmitter or receiver disappears over a hill.

Figure 7-3 is a model of a knife edge diffraction propagation situation. The most important thing to notice in this figure is that *the transmitter must be closer to the knife edge* (or to the real-life mountain ridge) *than the receiver.* Otherwise, the losses are very high.

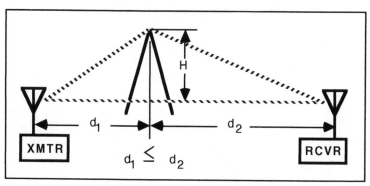

Figure 7-3 Knife Edge Diffraction Model

d_1 is the distance along the direct transmission path (i.e. if there were line of sight) from the transmitter to the point right below the knife edge. d_2 is the remaining distance to the receiver, and H is the height of the knife edge above what would otherwise be a line of sight path.

Figure 7-4 is a nomograph which gives the amount of additional loss (above the amount of loss if the link were line-of-sight). However, the chart is in terms of a calculated effective distance "d" which is a function of the propagation geometry. "d" is calculated from the formula:

$$d = \left[\frac{\sqrt{2}}{1 + \dfrac{d_1}{d_2}} \right] d_1$$

Here are a few values of d for typical cases:

If $d_2 = d_1$, $d = 0.7$ d_1
If $d_2 = 2.4\, d_1$, $d = d_1$
If $d_2 \gg d_1$, $d = 1.4\, d_1$

On the other hand, if you don't need accuracy greater than 1.5 dB, you can just use d_1 as the value of d in the nomograph. In real life, the inaccuracy caused by the shape of any obstruction you are trying to communicate over will probably be greater than ± 1.5 dB anyway.

To use the Figure 7-4 nomograph, draw a line from the distance factor (d) on the left hand scale through the knife edge height (H) on the second scale to the middle index line. Then, draw a line from the intersection of your first line through the operating frequency in MHz and on to the Loss in dB scale at the right. Be sure that the distance is in kilometers and that the height of the knife edge is in meters. (Appendix E includes equivalent charts for other units.)

The example in Figure 7-4 is for an effective distance (d) of 60 km and a knife edge height of 100 meters at 150 MHz. The knife edge diffraction loss would be approximately 10 dB above the free space attenuation. (Naturally, any appropriate atmospheric and rain attenuation must also be added.) Remember that the receiver cannot be closer to the knife edge than the transmitter, and that d is the effective distance. (e.g. d is 60 km if the transmitter is 60 km and the receiver is 144 km [2.4 x 60 km] from the knife edge.) We can just call d the distance from the transmitter to the ridge line if we only need accuracy to a couple of dB.

7-6

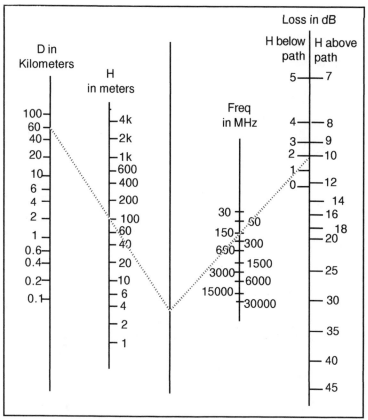

Figure 7-4 Knife Edge Diffraction Loss

Diffraction Loss over a Smooth Sphere

Figure 7-5 shows the attenuation (above line of sight spreading loss) that can be expected for transmission around a smooth spherical earth from low antennas. For antennas many wavelengths above the surface of the sphere, this will give about 2 dB too much loss.

In the example shown on the figure, a signal at 500 MHz transmitted 40 km over smooth earth would have about 12 dB of additional attenuation.

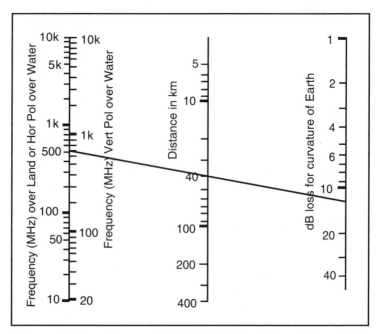

Figure 7-5 Diffraction Loss over Smooth Earth

7.3 Doppler Effect

When there is relative motion between a transmitter and a receiver, the received frequency is different from the transmitted frequency by a factor proportional to the relative velocity. Figure 7-6 shows a transmitter directly approaching a receiver, and the formula for the resulting change in frequency. Note that the received frequency is *greater* than the transmitted frequency because the transmitter is moving *toward* the receiver. Also note that it is only the rate of change of distance between the transmitter and receiver that matters. The same formula would apply if it were the receiver moving.

Figure 7-7 shows the more general case in which both the transmitter and receiver are moving in arbitrary directions. In this case, the relative velocity of the transmitter toward the receiver is the component of its

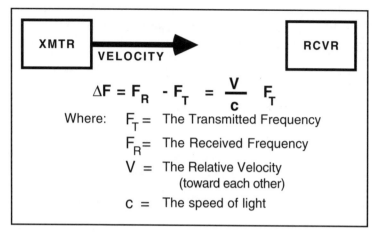

Figure 7-6 Doppler Effect

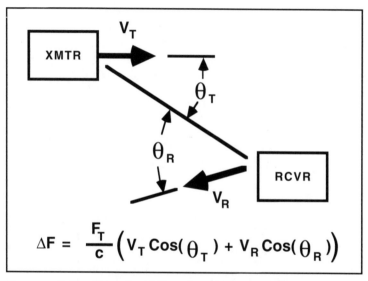

Figure 7-7 Doppler Effect for Arbitrary Velocity Vectors

velocity along the line connecting the transmitter and receiver (which = its velocity times the cosine of the angle between its velocity vector and the receiver. Likewise, the receiver's velocity must be reduced by the cosine of the angle between its velocity vector and the transmitter to find the component that contributes to the Doppler effect.

You will note that if the transmitter and receiver are directly approaching each other, the value of each cosine becomes one (1), so the relative velocity is the sum of the two velocities. This collapses the formula in Figure 7-7 to the formula in Figure 7-6.

If the transmitter and receiver are located together (as in a radar) and the signal reflects from an object with relative motion, the Doppler effect applies both to the outgoing and returning transmission paths. This is called the "two way Doppler effect," and the difference frequency is proportional to twice the relative velocity. For the two way Doppler case, just multiply the right side of each equation by two.

APPENDIXES

Appendix A

DERIVATION OF EQUATIONS AND CHARTS

The following derivations are included both to show the pedigree of some of the simplified equations in this book … and more important … to clearly identify the assumptions and rounding which have been applied.

kTB = -114 dBm/MHz

k = Bolzman's constant = 1.38×10^{-23} Joule/°K

T = 290°K

B = 1×10^6 Hz (units of Hz are 1/sec)

$$kTB = (1.38 \times 10^{-23})(290)(10^6) \frac{\text{Joule °K}}{\text{°K sec}}$$

$$= 4.002 \times 10^{-15} \text{ Watts} \quad (1 \text{ Watt} = 1 \text{ Joule/sec})$$

$$= (4.002 \times 10^{-15})(10^3) \frac{\text{watts milliwatts}}{\text{watt}}$$

$$= 4.002 \times 10^{-12} \text{ mW}$$

$10 \log(4.002 \times 10^{-12}) = -113.9772 \text{ dBm} \approx -114 \text{ dBm}$

Conversion of formulas from metric to other units

3.28 ft/m $\quad$ $10 \log(3.28) = 5.159$ dB ≈ 5.2 dB

1.6 km/mi $\quad$ $10 \log (1.6) = 2.04$ dB ≈ 2 dB

1.15 mi/nmi $\quad$ $10 \log (1.15) = .607$ dB $\approx .6$ dB

Spreading Loss = 32 x 20 log(F) x 20 log(d)

For frequency in MHz and distance in km

This formula is the ratio of the surface of a sphere of radius d (the distance from the isotropic transmitting antenna) and the effective area of the isotropic receiving antenna. The surface area of the sphere is $4\pi d^2$, and the receiving antenna area is $\lambda^2 / 4\pi$. The ratio of these two areas is then:

$$L_S = \frac{(4\pi)^2 \, d^2}{\lambda^2}$$

plugging in $\lambda = c/F$ gives:

$$= \frac{(4\pi)^2 \, d^2 \, F^2}{c^2} \frac{\sec^2 \, m^2}{m^2 \, \sec^2} = 1.755 \times 10^{-15}$$

Which is unitless as a well behaved ratio should be, but to input frequency in MHz and distance in km, we need to put in the conversion factors 10^3 m/km and 10^6 Hz/MHz. Both factors are squared and on the top, yeilding:

$$L_S = 1.755 \times 10^3 \, (\# \text{ of MHz})^2 \, (\# \text{ of km})^2$$

This converts to dB as: $32.44 + 20 \log(F) + 20 \log(d)$ which rounds to:

$$L_S = 32 + 20 \log(F) + 20 \log(d) \quad \text{for MHz \& km}$$

Using the unit conversion formulas on page A-1, the constant becomes $32.44 + (2.04 \times 2)$ (because of d^2) $= 36.52$ for distance in statute miles, so:

$$L_S = 37 + 20 \log(F) + 20 \log(d) \quad \text{for MHz \& sm}$$

and for distance in nautical miles, the constant becomes $36.52 + (.607 \times 2) = 37.734$ so:

$$L_S = 38 + 20 \log(F) + 20 \log(d) \quad \text{for MHz \& nm}$$

SQR in dB = 5 + 3(2m-1)

where an analog signal is digitized with m bits

The standard text book form of this equation is:

$$\frac{S}{N} = 3 \times 2^{(2m-1)}$$

Converting this to dB form gives:

$$10 \log(3) + (2m-1) \times 10 \log(2)$$
$$= 4.77 + 3(2m-1) \approx 5 + 3(2m-1) \quad \text{dB}$$

IF$_{FM}$ in dB = 5 + 20 log(ß)

For FM signals with RF SNR above threshold
The standard text book form of this equation (assuming proper filtering) is: $S_O/N_O = 3\ ß^2\ (S_{RF}/N_{RF})$.
The FM improvement factor is the ratio of the output and RF signal to noise ratios, or $3\ ß^2$.
Converting this to dB form gives: $10 \log(3) + 20 \log(ß)$
$$= 4.77 + 20 \log(ß) \approx 5 + 20 \log(ß)$$

Antenna area = 38.6 + G $\neq$ 20 log(F) dBsm

$$A = \frac{G\lambda^2}{4\pi}$$

Substituting $\lambda = c/F$ and 10^6 Hz/ MHz gives

$$A = \frac{c^2\ G}{4\pi\ F^2}\ \frac{m^2\ \sec^2}{\sec^2\ (10^6\ Hz\ /\ MHz)^2} = 7.162 \times 10^3\ \frac{G}{F^2}$$

Converting this into dB gives
$$A\ (dBsm) = 38.55 + G - 20\ Log(F)\quad \text{with F in MHz}$$

G = -42.2 + 20 log(D) + 20 log(F)   dB

Area of Isotropic Antenna $= \dfrac{\lambda^2}{4\pi}$

Area of Mouth of Dish Antenna $= \dfrac{\pi D^2}{4}$

The gain of the antenna is the ratio of the two areas $\quad = \dfrac{\pi^2 D^2}{\lambda^2} = \dfrac{\pi^2 F^2 D^2}{c^2}$

To factor in 55% efficiency and allow input of F^2 in MHz^2, this must be multiplied by the factor 0.55×10^{12} (D is already in meters)

Combining this with the numerical values of π and c (both squared) makes the equation

$$G = \frac{(5.5 \times 10^{11})\ (3.14159)^2}{(3 \times 10^8)^2}\ D^2 F^2 = 6.03 \times 10^{-5}\ D^2 F^2$$

Which converts to dB form as:
$$G = -42.2 + 20 \log(D) + 20 \log(F)$$

Antenna Gain (not in dB) = 29,000 / ($\theta_1 \times \theta_2$)

for 55% efficient antenna

The area of an elliptical area on a sphere is

two subtended
the sphere)

the area
antenna with
of θ_1 and θ_2 is:

equal to this
the gain of a
ing by .55
ntenna, so:

00

2

Noise Figure of Cascaded Stages

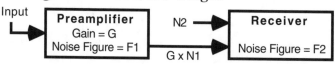

The noise figure (F) determines the noise (N) (above kTB) that if added at the input of a noiseless device would cause the measured output noise. This would require N1 into the preamplifer and N2 into the receiver to cause the measured noise at the receiver output. If all noise were injected at the "input," it would be (N2/G) + N1. This means that the system noise figure (at "input") is degraded from F1 by:

$$\text{Degradation} = \frac{N2/G + N1}{N1} = \frac{N2/G + N1}{N1} = \frac{N2}{G \times N1} + 1$$

This degradation factor is converted to dB form and plotted in Figure 6-5 and in Appendix D.

Appendix B

SIGNAL STRENGTH IN THE ETHER WAVES

It is common practice (including throughout this book) to state the signal strength of transmitted signals in dBm ... even though this makes no physical sense. dBm is a unit of electrical power, a ratio of the signal power to one milliwatt. Power is defined only within a circuit. After transmission from an antenna, signals are rigorously defined only in terms of field strength. The correct units are volts per meter (or more often microvolts per meter).

However, in many communication theory applications, it is extremely convenient to define a transmitted signal at some point in space in terms of dBm. That definition really assumes the situation shown in Figure B-1, in which an ideal unity gain antenna is located at the point in space being considered. The signal power in dBm is then the output of that ideal antenna at that location.

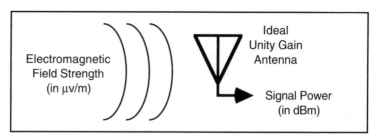

Figure B-1 Electromagnetic Field at an Antenna

Quick Conversion Formulas

The following equation will allow you to convert field density in microvolts per meter directly to the equivalent signal strength in dBm.

P = -77 + 20 log(E) - 20 log(F)

Where: P = Equivalent signal power (dBm)
E = Field strength (μv/m)
F = Frequency (MHz)

To convert the signal strength back into the equivalent field density, use the formula:

$$E = 10^{\left(\frac{P + 77 + 20 \log(F)}{20}\right)}$$

Derivation

In case you don't believe these formulas, or have a particular need to derive something, here is the derivation of the first equation.

The signal strength (i.e. output power) from the ideal antenna in Figure B-1 is defined by the formula:

$$P \text{ (watts)} = \frac{[E \text{ (v/m)}]^2 \; A \text{ (m}^2)}{Z_0 \text{ (ohms)}}$$

Where: P = Equivalent signal power
E = Field strength
A = Effective antenna area
Z_0 = Impedance of free space

The effective antenna area can be defined as a function of antenna gain by the following formula:

$$A = \frac{G \lambda^2}{2\pi} = \frac{G c^2}{4\pi F^2}$$

and the two constants are:

$$Z_0 \approx 120 \, \pi \text{ ohms} \qquad c = 3 \times 10^8 \text{ m/sec}$$

B-2

Setting the antenna gain equal to unity (i.e. 0 dB) and plugging the antenna area expression into the power equation gives:

$$P = \frac{(E^2)(c^2)}{(480\,\pi^2)(F^2)} \qquad \frac{\text{volts}^2 \quad \text{meter}^2}{\text{meter}^2 \quad \text{sec}^2\,(1/\text{sec})^2\,\text{ohms}}$$

$$= 1.8998 \times 10^{13}\,\frac{E^2}{F^2}\ \text{Watts} \qquad \text{(Combining all Units)}$$

But this gives the signal strength in watts and requires that the field density be input in volts/meter and the frequency in Hertz (not the most commonly used units). Multiplying the constant by the three factors:

$$10^{-12}\,v^2/\mu v^2$$

$$10^{-12}\,\text{MHz}^2/\text{Hz}^2 \quad \text{(The frequency term is on the bottom)}$$

$$10^3\,\text{mW/W}$$

yields the expression:

$$P(\text{in mW}) = 1.8998 \times 10^{-8}\,\frac{E\,(\mu v/m)^2}{F\,(\text{MHz})^2}$$

which, when converted to dB form using the formulas in Chapter 2 and rounding the constant to the nearest whole number becomes:

$$P = -77 + 20\,\log(E) - 20\,\log(F)$$

(Q.E.D, as the more pompous mathematicians say.)

Appendix C

QUICK FORMULAS FOR ANTENNAS

This appendix is a collection of formulas and nomographs which will allow you to select the appropriate antenna for any type of communications application. All are explained in Chapter 4, Section 4.4.

In this appendix:

G = Boresight gain (in dB unless otherwise noted)

A = Effective area in m^2, ft^2, dBsm, or dBsf

F = Frequency in MHz (or GHz on some charts)

D = Antenna diameter in meters or feet

θ_1 & θ_2 are the 3 dB beamwidths of an antenna in degrees in any mutually perpendicular planes

For a symmetrical parabolic dish antenna with 55% efficiency and diameter measured in *meters* :

$$G = -42.2 + 20 \ Log(D) + 20 \ Log(F)$$

If diameter is measured in *feet*, the formula is:

$$G = -52.6 + 20 \ Log(D) + 20 \ Log(F)$$

For a 55% efficient parabolic dish antenna:

$$\text{Gain (not in dB)} \approx \frac{29,000}{\theta_1 \, \theta_2}$$

For a 60% efficient horn antenna:

$$\text{Gain (not in dB)} \approx \frac{31,000}{\theta_1 \, \theta_2}$$

Effective Area of an antenna as a function of gain and frequency is:

$$A \ (\text{in dBsm}) = 38.6 + G - 20 \ log(F)$$
$$A \ (\text{in dBsf}) \ = 48.9 + G - 20 \ log \ (F)$$

C-1

Antenna Selection Criteria

Angular Coverage	Polar-ization	Band Width	Antenna Type
360° Azimuth	Linear	Narrow	Whip, Dipole, or Loop
		Wide	Biconical or Swastika
	Circular	Narrow	Normal Mode Helix
		Wide	Lindenblad or 4 Arm Conical Spiral
Directional	Linear	Narrow	Yagi, Array with Dipole Elements or Dish with Horn Feed
		Wide	Log Periodic, Horn or Dish with Log Periodic Feed
	Circular	Narrow	Axial Mode Helix or Horn with Polarizer or Dish with Crossed Dipole Feed
		Wide	Cavity Backed Spiral, Conical Spiral or Dish with Spiral Feed

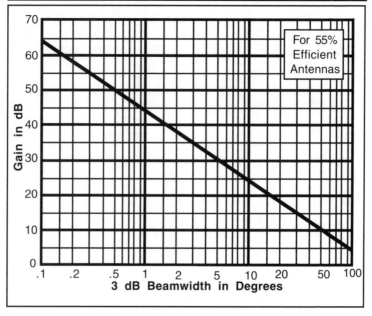

For 55% Efficient Antennas

Antenna Gain & Area (diameter in meters)

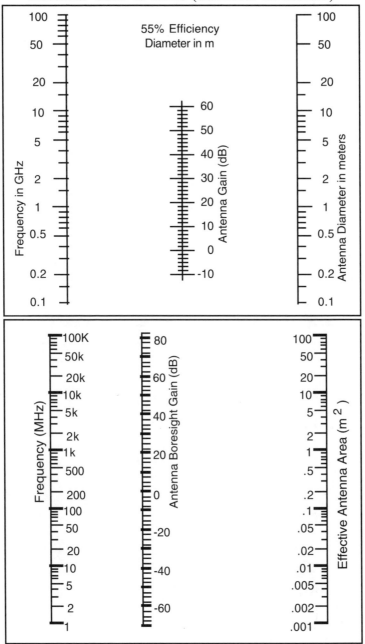

Antenna Gain and Area (diameter in feet)

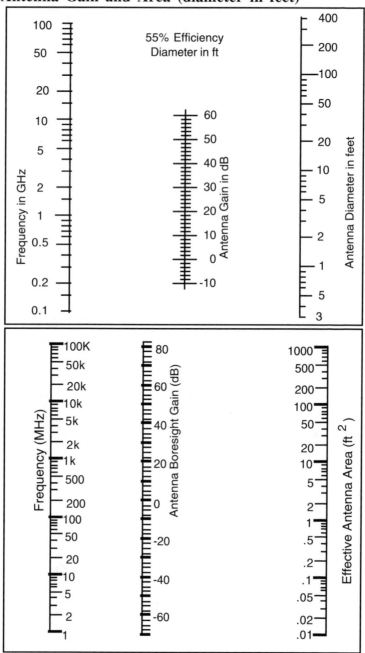

C-4

Antenna Gain Adjustment vs. Efficiency

Antenna Efficiency	Adjustment to Gain from 55% efficiency value
60%	Add 0.4 dB
50%	Subtract 0.4 dB
45%	Subtract 0.9 dB
40%	Subtract 1.4 dB
35%	Subtract 2 dB
30%	Subtract 2.6 dB

Antenna Polarization

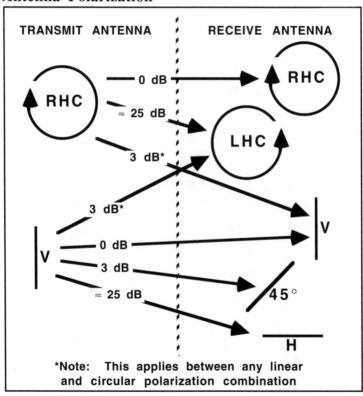

*Note: This applies between any linear and circular polarization combination

Appendix D

QUICK FORMULAS FOR RECEIVER SENSITIVITY

This appendix is a collection of formulas and nomographs which will allow you to calculate the sensitivity for a wide range of types of receivers and receiving systems. All are explained in Chapter 6.

Receiver Sensitivity (S) is the sum (in dB) of kTB, system noise figure (NF), and the required signal to noise ratio (SNR).

$$S = kTB + NF + SNR$$

At standard room temperature (290°K):

kTB = -114 dBm
+ 10 log [Receiver Bandwidth / 1 MHz)

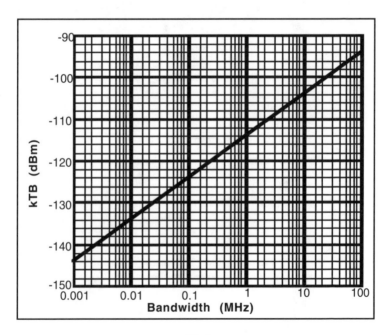

Noise Figure in Cascaded Stages

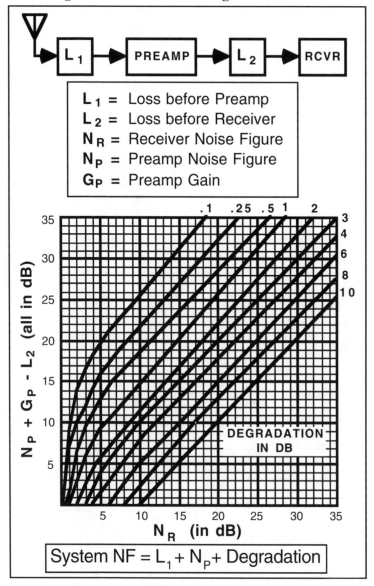

For FM signals, the output signal to noise ratio exceeds the RF signal to noise ratio by the improvement factor:

$$IF_{FM} = 5 + 20 \log(\beta)$$

as long as the RF SNR ≥ 12 dB for a conventional FM discriminator or 4 dB for a phase locked loop discriminator.

For digital signals, the signal to quantizing noise ratio for a signal digitized with m bits is:

SQR (in dB) = 5 + 3(2m-1)

Bits / Sample	Quantizing Levels	Equivalent SNR (in dB)
1	2	8
2	4	14
3	8	20
4	16	26
5	32	32
6	64	38
7	128	44
8	256	50
9	512	56
10	1024	62
11	2048	68
12	4096	74

Bit Error Rate vs. RF SNR

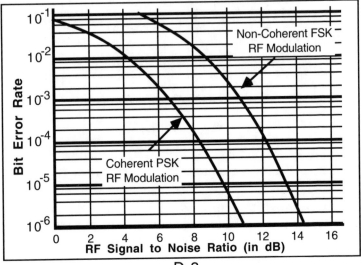

D-3

Appendix E

QUICK FORMULAS FOR PROPAGATION

This appendix is a collection of formulas and nomographs which will allow you to quickly calculate the signal strength at any point in a communication link -- in terms of the common link parameters. For each formula or chart, you can select link distance in kilometers (km), statute miles (sm), or nautical miles (nm). All are explained in Chapters 5 and 7. Abbreviations used are:

G_T = Transmitting antenna gain (dB)

G_R = Receiving antenna gain (dB)

P_T = Transmitter power (dBm)

ERP = Effective radiated power (dBm)

P_A = Power into receiving antenna (dBm)

P_R = Power into receiver (dBm)

L = All propagation losses (dB)
   $(L_S + L_{Atm} + L_{Rain} + L_{LOS})$

L_S = Spreading loss (dB)

L_{Atm} = Atmospheric loss (dB)

L_{Rain} = Loss from rain or fog (dB)

L_{LOS} = Loss from non-line-of-sight condition (dB)

F = Frequency (in MHz unless stated otherwise)

d = Distance from transmitter to receiver (various units)

H = Height (various units)

S = Sensitivity (dBm)   [S_{Rqd} = Required sensitivity]

M = Link margin (dB)

The Link Equation (several common forms)

$$P_R = P_T + G_T - L_S - L_{Atm} - L_{Rain} - L_{LOS} + G_R$$
$$P_R = ERP - L_S - L_{Atm} - L_{Rain} - L_{LOS} + G_R$$
$$P_R = ERP - L + G_R$$
$$P_A = ERP - L$$

Spreading Loss in dB is given by the following formulas:

For Frequency in MHz and Distance in kilometers (km):
$$L_S = 32 + 20 \log(F) + 20 \log(d)$$
For Frequency in MHz and Distance in statute miles (sm) :
$$L_S = 37 + 20 \log(F) + 20 \log(d)$$
For Frequency in MHz and Distance in nautical miles (nm):
$$L_S = 38 + 20 \log(F) + 20 \log(d)$$

Atmospheric Loss for various distance units
    This is the same chart presented in Chapter 5, however the loss in dB per statute mile (sm) or nautical mile (nm) can be found by extending the horizontal line out to the left hand scale.

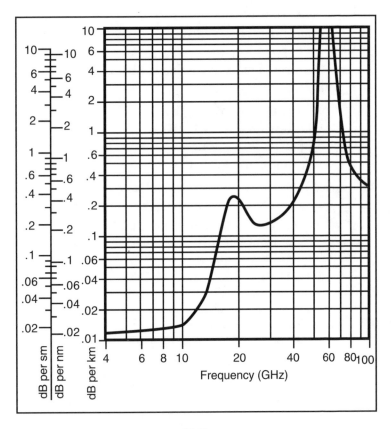

Atmospheric Loss Through Whole Atmosphere

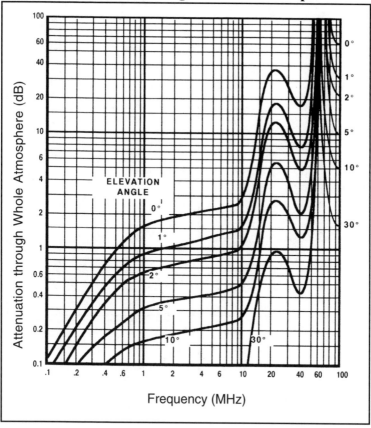

Attenuation through Whole Atmosphere (dB)

Frequency (MHz)

Knife edge propagation loss in the two nomographs on page 4 is based on the geometry shown below. Both show dB per unit distance vs. "**d**."

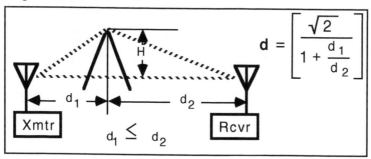

$$d = \left[\frac{\sqrt{2}}{1 + \dfrac{d_1}{d_2}} \right]$$

$d_1 \leq d_2$

Knife Edge Diffraction Loss above L_S

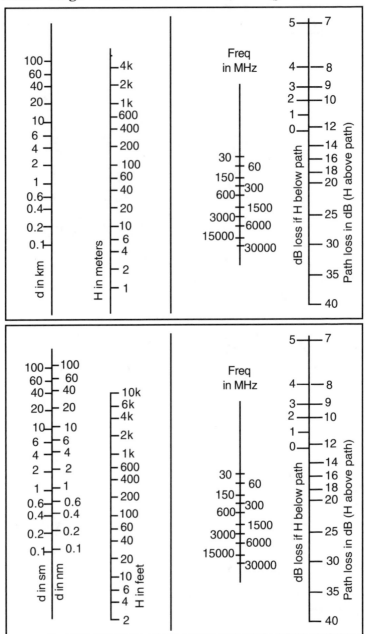

E-4

Additional Loss above L$_S$ from Curvature of Smooth Earth

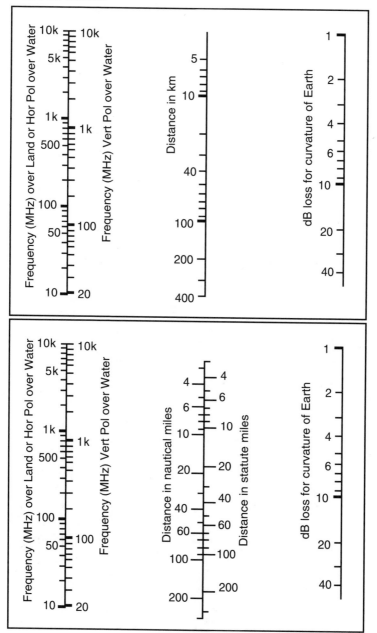

Spreading Loss (L$_S$) as a Function of Distance and Frequency

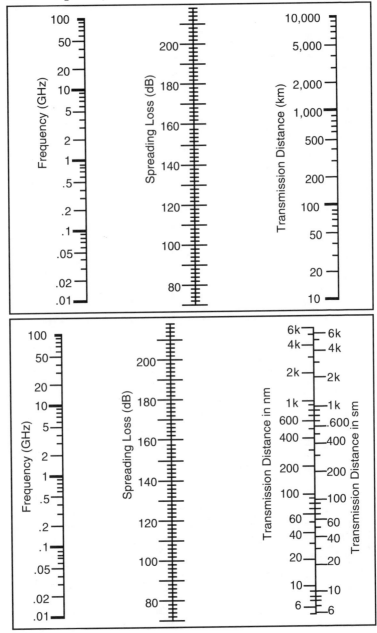

E-6

Attenuation from Rain or Fog

The attenuation lines on the charts on pages 7 and 8 are all defined by the tables at the bottom of this page.

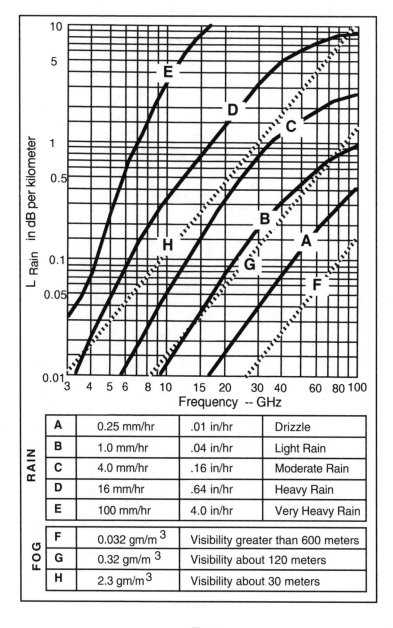

RAIN	**A**	0.25 mm/hr	.01 in/hr	Drizzle
	B	1.0 mm/hr	.04 in/hr	Light Rain
	C	4.0 mm/hr	.16 in/hr	Moderate Rain
	D	16 mm/hr	.64 in/hr	Heavy Rain
	E	100 mm/hr	4.0 in/hr	Very Heavy Rain
FOG	**F**	0.032 gm/m^3	Visibility greater than 600 meters	
	G	0.32 gm/m^3	Visibility about 120 meters	
	H	2.3 gm/m^3	Visibility about 30 meters	

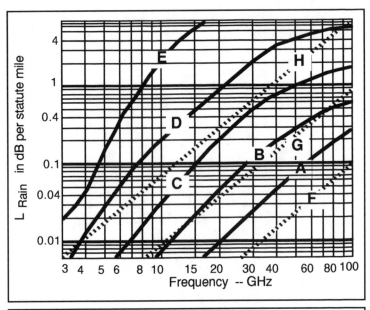

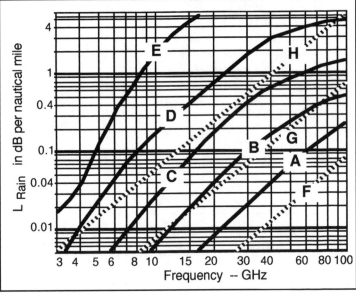

E-8

Link Relationship Formulas

Link Margin

$$M = P_R - S$$

Required Sensitivity

$$S_{Rqd} = ERP - 32 - 20 \log(F) - 20 \log (d)$$
$$- L_{Atm} + G_R - M \qquad \text{(for Distance in km)}$$

$$S_{Rqd} = ERP - 37 - 20 \log(F) - 20 \log (d)$$
$$- L_{Atm} + G_R - M \qquad \text{(for Distance in sm)}$$

$$S_{Rqd} = ERP - 38 - 20 \log(F) - 20 \log (d)$$
$$- L_{Atm} + G_R - M \qquad \text{(for Distance in nm)}$$

Effective Range

$$d = 10^{\left(\frac{20 \log(d)}{20}\right)} \qquad \textbf{Where:}$$

$20 \log(d) = ERP - S + G_R - L_{Atm} - M - 32 - 20 \log (F)$ for d in km

$20 \log(d) = ERP - S + G_R - L_{Atm} - M - 37 - 20 \log (F)$ for d in sm

$20 \log(d) = ERP - S + G_R - L_{Atm} - M - 38 - 20 \log (F)$ for d in nm

Interfering Signal to Desired Signal Ratio

$$I/S = ERP_I - ERP_S - L_I + L_S - I_A - I_F$$
(I_A is the antenna isolation in dB and I_F is the frequency filtering isolation in dB)

For in band interference with negligible difference in atmospheric attenuation

$$I/S = ERP_I - ERP_S - 20 \log(d_I) + 20 \log(d_S) - I_A$$

For out of band interference with negligible difference in atmospheric attenuation

$$I/S = ERP_I - ERP_S - 20 \log(d_I) + 20 \log(d_S)$$
$$- 20 \log(F_I) + 20 \log(F_S) - I_A - I_F$$

Appendix F

QUICK FORMULAS FOR DOPPLER SHIFT

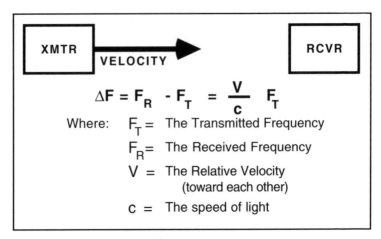

Figure F-1 Doppler Shift

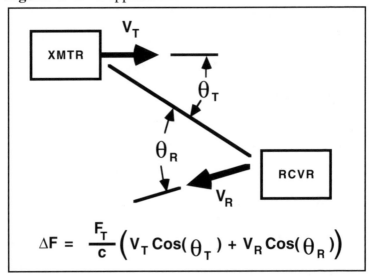

Figure F-2 Doppler Effect for Arbitrary Velocity Vectors

INDEX

ABOUT THE AUTHOR

You know perfectly well that authors write these "about the author" sections about themselves ... but write in the third person to somehow imply that an impartial third party is heaping on all that praise. As you will see while reading this book and then using it in your work, I have a great deal more respect for your intelligence and your valuable time than that.

The most important thing you should know about me is that I have actually used all of the working tools presented in this book ... out in the "hard cruel world" where making a large mistake usually costs your boss or your customer a lot of trouble and/or money. In a few cases, it has literally been a matter of life and death. I have also spent years as a technical manager of young, eager engineers who were (and are) a lot smarter than I ... but some of whom occasionally tried to defy the laws of physics in paper designs which were not always corrected before we built something that didn't do what our customers had a right to expect (... and which I enjoyed helping repair during many long nights.)

During over 30 years in the business, I have participated in the design, manufacture, testing and field support of a wide range of systems and subsystems which either transmit or receive radio signals in environments from submarines to space ... over frequency ranges from just above DC to just above light.

I hold a BSEE from Arizona State University and an MSEE from the University of Santa Clara, both with majors in communication theory, and have published dozens of articles on communications related topics in a variety of technical magazines and journals, including extensive tutorial sections in various handbooks. I have never published an integral sign ... all of these articles and tutorial sections have explained communication phenomenon using the same practical, application oriented approach used throughout this book.

I now make my living as owner of a small company that performs communications related design studies for large companies and the government. I also teach short courses all over the world on a variety of subjects for which a practical understanding of radio propagation is essential. In fact, the real reason for this book is that so many people in those classes found the techniques presented uniquely useful to them.

If you need a referral to an expert in a related field, or want one of my overview reports on related subjects (direction finding, spread spectrum, etc.) ... or just want to brag about a clever calculation technique to an appreciative colleague ... I would enjoy hearing from you. I can be reached at Lynx Publishing, 1587 Vireo Avenue, Sunnyvale, CA 94087. My phone (and fax) number is (408)747-0588. One never knows how long a book will be around ... and I will move to a consulting practice by a fishing stream in the hills one of these years ... so if your letter comes back, send it to P.O. Box 70544, Sunnyvale, CA 94086-0544. I promise to keep the P.O. box open to forward mail to that fishing stream ... wherever it may be.

To order copies of this book or detailed overview reports on various communications related subjects, contact:

Lynx Publishing
1587 Vireo Ave
Sunnyvale, CA 94087

Phone or Fax (408)747-0588